Dr. Ted Baehr has done a beautiful job inspiring us all in his new book, *Reel to Real*. I am so proud to have won some of his Movieguide® awards, and I'm honored to recommend his amazing new book.

—**Dolly Parton,** singer/songwriter, producer, actress, and philanthropist

After nearly two decades working in Hollywood, I've found that the secular space did not hinder my spirituality but enhanced it. I've learned valuable lessons from my industry and my dear friend, Dr. Ted Baehr, who has proven that even films can enrich our daily walk with God. *Reel to Real: 45 Movie Devotions for Families* is a groundbreaking book that references movies that inspire. Just like the many parables we turn to in times of emotional crisis, Dr. Ted Baehr has compiled films that reflect the Word of God, and this too deserves to be on your nightstand!

—**DeVon Franklin,** CEO/Franklin Entertainment

Reel to Real presents forty-five days of daily inspiration providing valuable spiritual and emotional insights to be found in movies. As a producer of film and television, I am grateful that these devotions help to bridge the gap between the mass media of entertainment and those who have a desire to know God better. Our friend Dr. Ted Baehr has done a wonderful job.

—**Roma Downey,** award-winning actress and producer

Dr. Ted Baehr has done a wonderful job weaving powerful, beloved movies as illustrations to give insights into the principles of God's Word, to help our children grow in godly wisdom, discernment, and grace. What fun—families sharing great movies that children love to foster biblical values! *Reel to Real* is two thumbs up!

—**Kevin Sorbo,** actor, director, producer

Ted Baehr is on	s he has stood
for the best in t	uenced innu-
merable product.	nd talent. In

his new book, he opens his heart and shares with you some of the secrets of Hollywood's best movies in a very enriching manner. Don't miss *Reel to Real*.

> **—Bruce Wilkinson,** author of *The Prayer of Jabez* and president of Teach Every Nation

Reel to Real is a wonderful parents' devotional guide for engaging memorable films to convey the importance of God's Word. Jesus spoke in parables, and Ted speaks in movies! I commend to everyone Dr. Ted Baehr's *Reel to Real*.

> **—Sam Sorbo,** award-winning actress, writer, and producer

Thank you, Ted Baehr, for helping us see movies through a "redemptive" lens. As a talk show host and parent, I know this book will be a valuable resource. So, two thumbs up—and they both point to the Savior! What a breath of fresh air and a "front-row" look at Hollywood from a true insider, yet through the beautiful perspective of eternity. This book should be in the homes of every family concerned with reaching our culture with the gospel of Jesus Christ!

> **—Stu Epperson Jr.,** president of The Truth Network and author of *First Words of Jesus*

My dear friend Ted Baehr is like John the Baptist, "a voice crying in the wilderness"! I've lived and worked in that wilderness—the entertainment world—for over fifty years now, and it has become truly an environment of great accomplishment but lost purpose … and lost souls. It is increasingly a "wilderness" of immorality, greed, and secular idolatry. But, for many of those same years, Ted Baehr has been revealing the good and the bad, the positive and destructive, in movies and television, helping guide parents and their children through the glittering morass of a cinematic "Never, Never Land" that glamorizes decadence but can eat away the morals of the young. And, as he annually shows how family-values entertainment has the best chance of profitability, his "Teddy Bear" awards are gratefully accepted by some of Hollywood's most successful writers, directors, producers, and stars. He's making a serious difference, and convincing many in the entertainment world that good can be more profitable and more award worthy than bad. And now comes this amazing book, the result of Ted's long study of the best and worst in films and TV—and his simultaneous immersion in the eternal Word of God. As Jesus used parables—stories of contemporary life—to teach everlasting truths, Ted Baehr is using contemporary films to illustrate and underscore vital lessons and moral guidance for young viewers! Every point is Scripture-based and every lesson obvious and undeniable. What an incredible asset for today's responsible parents! A personal example: When *The Exorcist* hit the screens, I took my young children to see it, hoping it would accurately depict real-life demonic activity in our day. And though it wasn't totally scriptural in all details, it so impacted my four young daughters that we prayed together as never before, not just then but through years to come. It made us realize that we are living in a spiritual battlefield, a literal war for our souls, and that belonging to God is our only way to navigate through the "wilderness" of modern life. Thank God for Ted Baehr, our valiant "voice crying in the wilderness"!

—**Pat Boone,** singer, composer, actor, writer, motivational speaker, and spokesman

In a world where people are actually perishing for lack of knowledge, all is not lost. Ted Baehr provides truth, encouragement and faith with life-affirming agape love in *Reel to Real: 45 Movie Devotions for Families.* This anecdotal, power-packed devotional imparts a godly path to world transformation in media and entertainment. A must read!

—**Evangelist Alveda King,** civilrightsfortheunborn.com

It gives me great pleasure to congratulate my good friend, Ted Baehr, on his new book *Reel to Real: 45 Movie Devotions for Families*. Ted has taken the movies of our day—the new parables of our culture—and gleaned important spiritual, emotional, and physical insights that can improve our lives and the lives of our families. He has relied on his extensive experience in entertainment media and his great love of God's Word to bridge the gap between the entertainment industry and the desire to know God and live for Him. I applaud Dr. Ted Baehr for the wonderful work he has done and am honored to recommend to you his newest success, *Reel to Real*.

—**Dr. M. G. "Pat" Robertson,** founder/chairman,
The Christian Broadcasting Network, Inc.

Dr. Ted Baehr has supported me and my passion to bring roles to life throughout the years. I am so excited for his book *Reel to Real: 45 Movie Devotions for Families* to be brought to the hearts and homes of many! Movies and entertainment create and drive our culture, so showing powerful insights into the principles in God's Word with movies as illustrations provide a bridge to help us grow in godly wisdom, discernment, and grace.

—**Bailee Madison,** star actress

Ted Baehr has used his years of experience in the world of film and entertainment to point us to the Word of God. Kudos for highlighting biblical life-lessons that can be gleaned from movies!

—**Alex Kendrick,** writer, producer, director, and actor

Make no mistake about it, movies often influence our culture greatly, often in unbiblical ways. Therefore, showing powerful insights into the principles in God's Word, with entertaining movies as illustrations, provides a bridge to help us and our children grow to be culture-wise and to redeem the mass media of entertainment. Therefore, I want to recommend Dr. Ted Baehr's *Reel to Real*.

—**James Garlow,** senior pastor of Skyline Church,
San Diego, California

REEL TO REAL

45 MOVIE DEVOTIONS FOR FAMILIES

DR. TED BAEHR

BroadStreet
PUBLISHING

BroadStreet Publishing® Group, LLC
Savage, MN, USA
BroadStreetPublishing.com

REEL TO REAL: *45 MOVIE DEVOTIONS FOR FAMILIES*

ISBN 978-1-4245-5610-6 (softcover)
ISBN 978-1-4245-5611-3 (e-book)

Stock or custom editions of BroadStreet Publishing titles may be purchased in bulk for educational, business, ministry, fundraising, or sales promotional use. For information, please email info@broadstreetpublishing.com.

Cover by MOVIEGUIDE®
Interior by Katherine Lloyd at theDESKonline.com

Printed in the United States of America
18 19 20 21 22 5 4 3 2 1

This book is dedicated to my loving wife, Lili; our four incredible children, Jim, Peirce, Robby, and Evelyn; all my grandchildren; contributors Bruce, David, Jaime, Mary, and Rob; and my great staff: Ben, Celeste, Courtney, Evy, Jeremy, Jerry and Carrol, Lili, Maggie, Michael and Kim, Nicole, Robby, Stephanie, and Tom.

Contents

Glad to Have the Light:
Of the Bible and the Screen

In 1946, at the height of the Golden Age of Hollywood, I was born to Theodore Baehr (whose stage name was Robert "Tex" Allen) and Evelyn Peirce, both of whom were successful stage, screen, and television actors. Growing up in New York, I followed in my parents' footsteps, performing in commercials, movies, television, and stage.

My parents were stars, but few remember them today, even though my father won the Box Office Award in 1936. Fame is fleeting.

While my parents were wonderful people, my mother died when I was young, and I ended up setting out on the wrong path—looking for love in all the wrong places and practicing self-destructive and leftist behavior. In the early 1970s, I put together the legal work to help a friend start a movie company. As is often the case in the entertainment industry, this friend didn't have the money to pay me, so I had to find the investor in the five-picture deal so they could pay me for my work. Then, in the midst of film financing, a wonderful older woman gave me a Bible and said, "Show me the errors in the Bible."

As I tried to find fault with His written Word, God showed me what I needed and turned my life right side up. Suddenly I understood John 10:10, where Jesus says, "The thief comes only to steal and kill and destroy. I came that they may have life and have it abundantly" (ESV). On the day I came to Christ in 1974, the drugs stopped, the philandering stopped, and the looking for love in all the wrong places stopped. Jesus set me free and gave me a more abundant life.

God is the Author and the Creator, and He turned on the light and everything changed. That makes me glad to have the light—both the light to see that there's good and evil and to know the difference between the two, as well as the light of movies that illumines biblical truth.

Filled with the Holy Spirit by faith in Jesus Christ, I attended seminary. Tuition needed to be paid, so I accepted a position as Director of the Television Center at the City University of New York (CUNY); was Director of TV and Radio at Trinity Church, Wall Street; and started the Good News Communications ministry (in 1978).

At CUNY I worked closely with academia, researching and testing the impact of the mass media of entertainment on cognitive development, and helping to perfect one of the first media-literacy curriculums. I was elected president of the Episcopal Radio & Television Foundation in 1979 and began conceptualizing another ministry, the Christian Film & Television Commission®. During my tenure, the Episcopal Radio & Television Foundation won an Emmy Award for Best Animated Special for *The Chronicles of Narnia: The Lion, the Witch, and the Wardrobe*, which aired on CBS and was watched by more than 37 million viewers. I was nominated for another Emmy Award for the PBS series *Perspectives: War and Peace*, in which I served as the executive producer, creative director, and host.

My previous research into the influence of the mass media of entertainment became a primary topic for my talk on "Television & Reality" at the Conference on Culture and Communication convened by Dr. Stewart Hoover at Temple University (1981). At the conference I received national recognition.

In 1983, while I was serving on the Communications Board

of the National Council of Churches and the National Religious Broadcasters, the great movie producer Ken Wales (*The Pink Panther* and *Christy*) introduced me to George Heimrich and his work at the now-defunct Protestant Film Office. Inspired by George and his beloved wife, Lucille, I began contacting prominent members of the entertainment industry and, in 1985, formed the Christian Film & Television Commission® ministry and Movieguide®: The Family Guide to Movies and Entertainment.

George Heimrich donated his Protestant Film Office files to the ministry, which uses the same vision for positive change to redeem the values of the mass media of entertainment according to biblical principles. It does this by influencing key entertainment executives to adopt higher standards and by informing and equipping the public, especially parents with children and families.

Part of the reason for the breakdown of morality in movies and television today, and in the culture at large, is that people of faith have retreated from being salt and light in the culture. From 1933 to 1966, Christians were a predominant force in Hollywood. During those years, the Roman Catholic Legion of Decency and the Protestant Film Commission (formed several years after the Legion of Decency) read every script to ensure that movies represented the largest possible audience by adhering to high standards of decency. As a result, *Mr. Smith [Went] to Washington*, *It [Was] a Wonderful Life*, and *The Bells of St. Mary's* rang out across the land!

It took approximately ten years and God's grace, acting through three dedicated Christian men, to position God's people to be such a powerful moral influence on Hollywood. As the documentary *Hollywood Uncensored* all too clearly demonstrates, prior to the involvement of these Christian men in 1933, American movies were morally bankrupt—full of nudity, perversity, and violence. From 1922 to 1933, churchgoing men and women tried everything, including censorship boards, to influence Hollywood to make wholesome entertainment. Nothing succeeded until Christians volunteered to work alongside the Hollywood studios to help them reach the largest possible audience.

When the Protestant Film Office closed its advocacy offices in Hollywood in 1966 (in spite of many pleas not to by top Hollywood filmmakers), not only did it open the floodgates to violence (*The Wild Bunch*), sex and satanism (*Rosemary's Baby*), and perverse anti-religious bigotry (*Midnight Cowboy*, the first X-rated movie to win a Best Picture Oscar), but it also caused a severe drop in movie attendance, from 44 million tickets sold per week to about 20 million.

As a result of my conversations with Sir John Templeton beginning in 1988, the Christian Film & Television Commission® ministry initiated the Annual Movieguide® Faith & Values Awards Gala and Report to the Entertainment Industry in 1992 and 1993 in Los Angeles.

The gala now features the prestigious Epiphany Prizes for the Most Inspiring Movie and TV Program that help people know God and understand Him better; the Faith & Freedom Awards for Promoting Positive American Faith & Values; the Kairos Prize for Spiritually Uplifting Screenplays by First-Time and Beginning Screenwriters; the Kairos Pro Prize for Spiritually Uplifting Screenplays by Established Screenwriters; the Annual Grace Awards for the Most Inspiring Performances in Movies & TV, given to the two actors/actresses whose performances best display God's grace and mercy toward us as human beings; and the Movieguide® Teddy "The Good News" Bear Awards for the Ten Best Movies for Families and the Papa Bear Awards for the Ten Best Movies for Mature Audiences. I seek to acknowledge those movies, TV programs, and actors/actresses truly deserving of praise, and those persons responsible for bringing them to the screen.

To add glamour to the event, actors and actresses are invited to host and be presenters of the awards. Music and entertainment are added to make it a memorable event, and we also hand out Bibles and other redemptive materials to carry out our mission to reach Hollywood for Christ.

Within the context of an elegant affair, I present Movieguide®'s Report to the Entertainment Industry. Through careful analysis of box office figures and Movieguide® criteria on 99 percent of movies released in two hundred theaters or more, including all major movies released by the seven Hollywood entertainment-industry studios, I give valuable and unique information to the highest-level Hollywood leaders, filmmakers, and talents through an impactful presentation. The purposes of the gala and the report are:

- To encourage filmmakers to continue to make movies with moral and spiritually uplifting values;
- To share the concerns of the majority of the American public in regard to the negative influences of today's movies; and
- To present an in-depth study of the annual movie box office and to not only dispel myths that extreme sex, violence, and nudity sell, but also to show that family movies and movies with morally uplifting Christian values and positive Christian content make the most money by far.

When we started Movieguide® in 1985, Hollywood's major studios released few major movies with any positive Christian content or values—less than 2 percent. But by the time we started the Annual Movieguide® Faith & Values Awards Gala and Report to the Entertainment Industry in 1992 and held the first Gala luncheon in 1993, there were 27 such movies, or about 10.38 percent of the market share. Incredibly, twenty-five years later in 2016, at least 184, or 63.88 percent, of major movies released by the industry contained at least some positive Christian, redemptive content. That's a numerical increase of 581 percent and a percentage increase of 515 percent!

Also, when we started in 1985, less than 6 percent of major movies were aimed at families. In the past several years, movies marketed to families have increased to nearly 40 percent of the top movies released in local theaters. As well, there were only about one or two movies being made with strong, explicit Christian content or values in 1985, but now there are sixty-seven or more such movies each year. That's at least a 3,250 percent increase.

The former chairman of a major Hollywood studio told me that he attributed all these positive shifts directly to Movieguide®'s influence and the Christian Film & Television Commission's box office analysis and annual report to the entertainment industry. Many major movie studios now have a Christian faith-based film division, and several studios are producing major movies with strong or overt Christian or biblical content. As well, all the major studios, not just Disney, are putting out movies for young children and families.

Of course, this doesn't mean that the studios aren't doing bad movies anymore, but it does mean there are fewer and fewer of these movies, and an increasing number of good ones. It's our prayer that the movie industry will increasingly make more commendable movies, and remove offensive elements from them.

Clearly, the work of Movieguide® and the Christian Film & Television Commission® ministry, especially our Annual Movieguide® Faith & Values Awards Gala and Report to the Entertainment Industry, has helped significantly to restore the values of the entertainment industry. Many studio executives and entertainers are getting the message. More good movies are being made each year, and Hollywood is being redeemed. Even so, the most powerful people in the entertainment industry are the people who buy the movie tickets. If they support good movies, then the good will do well.

WHY REEL TO REAL

Movies and entertainment have become the primary cultural influence of our civilization and teacher of our youth. Many sociologists have pointed out that movies and entertainment have replaced community, education, and religion in many areas as the touchstone for faith and values. However, the faith and values proclaimed in movies and entertainment often are not conducive in building sound minds, hearts, and bodies, as well as our culture and our future.

Movies and entertainment are a tool of communication. Tools can be used for good (to build a house) or for bad (to tear it down). *Reel to Real* looks at critical biblical principles using great, uplifting movies and entertainment to illustrate those principles God has given us. It directs people to movies that build up and instill principles that give a more abundant life. It is our hope that *Reel to Real* helps individuals and families develop discernment, wisdom, and a deeper understanding of God's Word. This is a great opportunity to reach youth of all ages who are immersed in the mass media of entertainment.

PREPARATION FOR STUDY

Proverbs 2:6 says: "For the LORD gives wisdom; from His mouth come knowledge and understanding" (HCSB). God speaks to us even from a burning bush. Hearing His voice revealing truth to give us wisdom is a blessing from Him. Here are a few steps for success in utilizing this book:

1. Decide to commit

You can use this book in two ways. One way is to watch the movies mentioned at the beginning of each devotion, read through the devotion, and then move to the questions and prayer, which are designed to help you pull from the films a life application for you and your family. Or, if you have already seen a movie mentioned and recall its details, you can go right to the main part of the devotion and then to the questions and prayer.

You can work through this book over the next several weeks, or you can take months or even a year or more, depending on the time available to you. What's most important is that you do not give up seeking wisdom, knowledge, and understanding for yourself and your family—and that you commit to using this devotional to enrich and inspire your life with God.

2. Pick a time

Choose a time that will work best with your schedule.

3 Read and watch

Carefully read the devotion and the Bible verses and watch the referenced movies. Information about each movie can also be found at movieguide.org.

4. Journal

Answer the closing questions, then write out anything you hear from God or feel you need to contemplate.

5. Pray

Allow time to speak with God and tell Him everything you would tell a best friend. If you have never invested in personal prayer, making this decision could revolutionize your spiritual growth.

7. Listen and obey

Close your time with a quiet moment to hear God speak. Then obey what you hear He tells you each day. The goal is to complete these devotions and allow Jesus to change your life.

May God bless you as you devote yourself to *Reel to Real*.

What Is God's Purpose for Your Life?

On occasion (or often), you may ask yourself, *What is my purpose in life? What is God's purpose for my life? What am I doing? Why am I doing it?* This may especially happen when you're exhausted and stressed.

These questions arise in movies too, such as in Frank Capra's masterful *It's a Wonderful Life*, in which God uses an angel-in-training to help George Bailey understand his purpose, and *Smurfs: The Lost Village*, in which Smurfette finds that giving her life for others (and being resurrected) is her purpose in life.

If you turn to God's Word, you'll find it has some encouraging news. While some people in the Bible (like Moses and David) received step-by-step instructions from God, most of us don't. But He does give us an incredible plan for our life, which we can find in 1 Thessalonians 5:16–18.

Before we get into that Scripture, though, let's look at John 10:10. Jesus says that the thief comes to kill, steal, and destroy, but that He came to set us free and give us an abundant life. Think about it—an abundant life. What does that mean?

For George Bailey, a more abundant life didn't mean traveling the world and becoming rich and famous, but it did mean rescuing the Savings and Loan (to help others have an abundant life) and having a wonderful wife, family, and friends. For Smurfette, a more abundant life didn't mean becoming the town grouch or getting a name that identified what she did; rather, it meant warning the lost village of Smurfs and giving up her life to save them from the evil wizard.

Now back to 1 Thessalonians 5:16–18. When my first son, Peirce, was only a few years old, I was preaching on this passage and thought, *What do I want for my son out of his life? Do I want him to follow in my footsteps and go to Dartmouth College and Cambridge University and do all the things I've done? Do I want him to go to New York University School of Law and practice law?*

That was when I realized that I want for him (and my other two sons and daughter) what God wants for us: "Always be happy. Never stop praying. Give thanks whatever happens. That is what God wants for you in Jesus Christ" (1 Thessalonians 5:16–18 ICB). I wanted (and still want) my children to be happy, to talk to me (and they usually do—most of the time), and to have an attitude of gratitude so they can appreciate those around them and what God has done in their lives.

Now look at how the passage ends: "That is what God wants for you in Jesus Christ." No other place in the Bible tells in such clear words what God's will is for us: to be happy, to talk to Him, and to be grateful. What a wonderful plan for our life!

For George Bailey, God's will was for him to have an attitude of gratitude by realizing he had a "wonderful life." For Smurfette, God's will was for her to have an attitude of gratitude for being created to do something no other Smurf could do. So, in a fallen world with trials and tribulations, "Rejoice always, pray continually, give thanks in all circumstances; for this is God's will for you in Christ Jesus."

You will then discover that yours is a wonderful life.

FILM TO FAITH

Watch one or both of these movies:

- *It's a Wonderful Life*
- *Smurfs: The Lost Village*

Ask:

- How did each hero or heroine discover God's perfect will for their life?
- How did they talk to God?
- How did they hear God?
- How did they: Rejoice? Pray? Give thanks?
- How can you put into practice God's will for your life?
- How do you: Rejoice? Pray? Give thanks?

Father, I rejoice when I recall all the good in my life. I ask you for direction in fulfilling your will for my life, and thank you for the blessings you bestow on me in Jesus Christ's name by the power of the Holy Spirit.

LOOKING AHEAD

Do you need strength for all you have to do and want to do? See the next devotion.

The Joy of the Lord
Is Your Strength

MOVIES THAT INSPIRE

Sing
Les Misérables (mature audiences)
Squanto: A Warrior's Tale

Do you need strength for all you have to do and want to do?

Nehemiah 8:10 says that "the joy of the LORD is your strength." And we all need strength. I need it quite often—when I'm trying to excel, when I'm doing my work, when I'm writing movie reviews, and when I'm talking to studio executives in Hollywood.

In the wonderful, animated, family movie *Sing*, a koala named Buster Moon needs strength to put on a singing competition to save his failing theater. In *Les Misérables*, Jean Valjean needs strength to escape his past and live a transformed life so he can raise orphaned Cosette. And in *Squanto: A Warrior's Tale*, the Pilgrims need strength to survive in the dangerous wilderness of the New World.

In the case of the remnant of Jews, who returned from captivity in Babylon and rebuilt the walls of Jerusalem, they needed strength to overcome their fear after Ezra read the Law that God had given them, which they realized they had failed to keep. So Nehemiah offered them joyous strength.

Just where do we find the strength that flows from real joy? By doing what Jesus called us to do.

Now Jesus called us to do a lot. He called us to love our neighbor as ourselves (Matthew 22:39). He called us to love God with all our heart, mind, and soul (Matthew 22:37). He also called us, as Paul reminds us in 1 Corinthians 11:23–27, to remember Jesus' redemptive sacrifice for us by partaking in communion and giving thanks for his death and resurrection that delivered us from the shackles of sin. Paul is telling us to give thanks for the fact that Jesus Christ set us free.

I do thank Jesus! He set me free from a debauched lifestyle. I grew up in the entertainment industry without the knowledge of His love, forgiveness, and ultimate freedom, but Jesus set me free in a day, and I've never looked back.

The early Greek-speaking Christians called communion the "great thanksgiving" or the *Eucharist*. I love this Greek word because it's made up of three little words, kind of like nesting dolls. Inside the act of Eucharist (or "thanksgiving") is the Greek word *charis*, which means "gift," and in the heart of the word *charis* is the Greek word *chara*, which means "joy."

In other words, the strength of the "joy of the LORD" is found in thanksgiving, not in weeping about what you didn't do, as the Jews were doing in Nehemiah. The strength of the "joy of the LORD" is a gift you get when you're giving thanks that Jesus did what you could not: He fulfilled the law to set you free.

This is the joy that Buster found when he heard the shy elephant girl singing "Hallelujah." It is the joy that Jean Valjean found when he gave thanks for the bishop showing him the love, mercy, and forgiveness of Jesus Christ and when he thanked God for Cosette. And this is the joyous strength that the Pilgrims found when they celebrated the first Thanksgiving with their Native American neighbors.

Where can you find the "joy of the LORD" that gives you the strength to do all that God has called you to do? By giving thanks for Jesus' death and resurrection on the cross, which set you free to live a more abundant life. This is a wonderful gift that Jesus tells us to do as often as we eat and drink.

Do you need strength to face today and tomorrow? A good place to start is to give thanks to receive the "joy of the LORD," as we do as believers in the "great thanksgiving."

FILM TO FAITH

Watch one or more of these movies:

- *Sing*
- *Les Misérables* (mature audiences)
- *Squanto: A Warrior's Tale.*

Ask:

- How did each hero discover real joy?
- How did each hero discover the joyous strength of thanksgiving?
- How can you put into practice giving thanks to God to receive the gift of the "joy of the LORD" that is your strength?
- How did you receive the gift of freedom and abundant life from Jesus Christ?
- How are you living in thanksgiving?

Father, I give you thanks for everyone and everything in my life, and for all the blessings you have bestowed on me [list some of these blessings] in Jesus Christ's name by the power of the Holy Spirit.

LOOKING AHEAD

Do you love to tell your friends about your favorite sports team, movie, and/or friend? See the next devotion.

Go and Tell
the Greatest Story

MOVIES THAT INSPIRE
God's Not Dead 2
Amazing Grace

Do you love to tell your friends about your favorite sports team, movie, and/or friend? Most of us like to talk about what we love. For me, having been saved by Jesus Christ from the depraved entertainment-industry lifestyle, I love to witness about His grace that set me free.

But it was not always this way. In the beginning of my journey with Jesus in the mid-1980s, I found witnessing difficult, as many Christians do. "Doing church" was more appealing to me—going from one worship service to another and then even seminary.

In Acts 1:8, Jesus, before ascending into heaven, tells his disciples, "But you will receive power when the Holy Spirit has come on you, and you will be My witnesses" (HCSB). He doesn't say "you *could* be," "you *should* be," or "you *might* be My witnesses"; Jesus proclaims, "You *will* be My witnesses." He then continues, "in Jerusalem, in all Judea and Samaria, and to the ends of the earth." Just a few days afterward, the disciples were filled with the Holy Spirit, their signal that they should go and witness "to the ends of the earth."

God doesn't give His disciples much choice here. When filled with His Holy Spirit, we will witness about His good news to the world. That is Jesus Christ's final instruction to us.

So did the disciples immediately set out to get to the sometimes hard, sometimes scary work of witnessing? No. They hung around the temple in Jerusalem for the next seven chapters. It wasn't until Acts 8:1 that they went to do what Jesus called them to do. Instead, they responded as if the temple were still the center of their faith, and they didn't believe they had the power for the work God had given them. It took the persecution that begins in Acts 8 to wake them up, when they're driven into Judea, Samaria, and the ends of the earth, except for the apostles.

God is omnipotent, or all-powerful, so He could have stopped the persecution. He is also omniscient, so He could have warned the believers. But He did neither. One can only conclude that because the disciples wouldn't do what He told them to do, God allowed the persecution. He let them be driven out of Jerusalem.

This handful of disciples began turning the Roman Empire right side up, from the most wicked and cruel kingdom to a civilized community of law that even finally abolished the evil entertainment of the gladiatorial games. The disciples were filled with power to be Jesus Christ's witnesses. It wasn't the power of man; it was the power of God for the work of witnessing.

God deserves all the praise. The disciples didn't have to change anyone. Only the Holy Spirit can change hearts. As His disciples, we merely need to obey Jesus' commands and tell the greatest story ever told. God will empower us to do it.

Consider what happens in the movie *God's Not Dead 2*. Grace Wesley (played by Melissa Joan Hart), a public school teacher, keeps her faith to herself until she's asked a question by a student. This demands an honest answer about Jesus, who she notes turned the other cheek and gave His life for other people. After responding honestly, Grace faces severe persecution and has to find the power of God's grace to stand up and witness to the gospel of Jesus Christ.

In the movie *Amazing Grace*, William Wilberforce comes to Jesus Christ and is transformed from a bon vivant into an amazing Christian who soon goes to ask John Newton if he should remain in Parliament or become a pastor. Newton tells Wilberforce that his ministry is in Parliament. By staying in Parliament, Wilberforce faces severe opposition, but even so becomes one of the greatest witnesses to the truth of the gospel.

Jesus tells us we will be empowered to be His witnesses. How? By humbly trusting Him and asking the Holy Spirit to empower us to witness. Jesus knows what He's called us to do, and He will give us the power we need through the Holy Spirit to do the work He commissioned.

Trust, and then tell everyone the good news that Jesus Christ came to set everyone free to live an abundant, eternal life with our divine Creator.

FAITH TO FILM

Watch one or both of these movies:

- *God's Not Dead 2*
- *Amazing Grace*

Ask:

- How did each hero or heroine find the power to witness?
- How did they witness to Jesus Christ?
- How did they overcome opposition?
- Whom did God transform with their witness?
- How have you been empowered to witness to the greatest story ever told?
- What has happened when you witnessed?

*Father, I love you and thank you for forgiving me and trans-
forming my life. Sometimes I don't go forth to tell others
about your good news. Please have your Holy Spirit empower me to go into all the world to be your witness. In Jesus
Christ's name, amen.*

LOOKING AHEAD

Do you contemplate the dichotomy between your thoughts and
your physical person? See the next devotion.

Both/And

Man of Steel
The Passion of the Christ (mature audiences)

Do you contemplate the dichotomy between your thoughts and your physical person? Have you asked if there is more to life—if this is all there is?

The answer to these questions may be found in the nature of reality designed by God that is "both/and," not "either/or." Consider, for example, how wonderful it is that Jesus is *both* fully God *and* fully man. He is not *either* just a man *or* just God; Jesus is "both/and."

We are told in John 1:1–3, 14, 18:

> In the beginning was the Word, and the Word was with God, and the Word was God. He was with God in the beginning. Through him all things were made; without him nothing was made that has been made. … The Word became flesh and made his dwelling among us. We have seen his glory, the glory of the one and only Son, who came from the Father, full of grace and truth. … No one has ever seen God, but the one and only Son, who is himself God and is in closest relationship with the Father, has made him known.

So Christianity is a "both/and" religion. While many unorthodox or heretical aberrations spring from an inability to grasp the "both/and," God's creation manifests it.

Recently, I was studying a course in astrophysics taught by the famous UC Berkeley professor Alex Filippenko. He spent one class showing that light is both energy and matter. To illustrate this simply, if you shine the subatomic nature of light through a latticework, it will appear to be a wave, but if you shine it through a point, it will appear to be a particle. Of course, the physics of this phenomena is much more complex, but the science of astrophysics teaches us that we live in a "both/and" universe.

Many comic-book-based movies are about heroes who are "both/and." The Superman comic and movies are overtly Christological, because the creators of the comic books, Jewish writer Jerry Siegel and artist Joe Shuster, wanted a popular Christ-like character as an alternative to Jesus Christ Himself. So, in this incomplete analogy, Clark Kent poses as human while Superman is the alien demigod (in contrast to this, Jesus is fully human and is fully God).

Man of Steel is actually one of the best of the Superman movies. When he's asked to surrender in the movie, Superman seeks answers in a Christian church. He tells the minister he knows he can't trust the villain General Zod, but he's not sure he can trust humans either. With a stained-glass picture of Jesus in the background, the minister tells Superman that sometimes you have to take a leap of faith and trust in someone.

Of course, Jesus movies also must have a hero who is "both/and." The 2004 movie *The Passion of the Christ* is Mel Gibson's masterpiece about the final hours of Jesus, which show both His humanity in suffering and His divinity in the resurrection. The movie covers the time period from the garden of Gethsemane to the cross and beyond. Unlike most Passion plays, it highlights in stark, dark, intense terms the spiritual warfare raging around Jesus Christ during his passion.

The first scene has Jesus weeping in the garden of Gethsemane, as satan, an androgynous figure accompanied by a snake, tries to tempt Jesus away from his destiny on the cross. Jesus rejects satan's temptation and crushes the snake's head with his foot (a visual reference to Genesis 3:15, which predicts that the Messiah will crush satan's head, the origin of sin). Soon thereafter, Judas leads the temple guards into the garden to arrest Jesus. From that point, the brutal treatment of the Messiah is shown in vivid detail. The violence and the glee of the Romans scourging Jesus highlight the demonic quality of the battle Jesus was fighting. Those who see the film will understand, perhaps for the first time, the price that Jesus paid to forgive us our sins.

Now some people, such as materialists, atheists, humanists, and communists, believe that matter is all there is. But if that is the case, then your life doesn't matter, because you are expendable like everything else. As a result, atheist regimes in the twentieth century (for example, Soviet Russia, Communist China, North Vietnam, North Korea, and Pol Pot in Cambodia) murdered about 153.3 million people for philosophical, political, and economic reasons.[1]

In contrast, according to the three-volume *Encyclopedia of Wars* by Charles Phillips and Alan Axelrod, religious wars account for only 7 percent, or 123 of the 1,763 wars in recorded human history, and more than 50 percent involved Islam, the so-called "religion of peace," even though Islam did not even exist as a religion for three thousand years of recorded human warfare.[2]

---

1 "Are Christianity and Religion the Biggest Evils in History?" *The Culture Watch*, February 29, 2016, accessed September 28, 2017, https://www.theculturewatch.com/are-christianity-and-religion-the-biggest-evils-in-history-2.

2 Charles Phillips and Alan Axelrod, *Encyclopedia of Wars*, vols. 1–3 (New York: Facts on File, 2004), and Rich Deem, "Religion and War: Are Most Wars the Result of Religious Belief?" http://www.godandscience.org/apologetics/war_and_religion.html.

Then another group of people, including some agnostics, occultists, and Hindus, say that everything is just an illusion. However, if everything is just an illusion, then your life doesn't matter, because you are illusory like everything else. Hindus contend that suffering is just *maya*, or an illusion, so when Mother Teresa was rescuing the dying off the streets of Calcutta, India, the Hindu leaders got angry. They tried to burn her to death on a funeral pyre because her actions meant that these destitute, suffering people were more than an illusion and had real value because they were all created in the image of the real God.

As Christians, we believe that we live in a world with real pain and real suffering and we need a real Savior. So we are both the material and the spiritual who are inextricably linked together in a wonderful way.

Now what does all that mean for *your* life?

It means you have infinite value, because you were created by God the Father as a unique being in His image, *and* you have infinite value, because the Creator God Himself, Jesus, died for you and rose from the dead to give you eternal life.

Christianity is a "both/and" religion. Being fully God and fully man, Jesus can bear the punishment for the transgressions of our humanity, and He can triumph over sin as the very Creator, God. There is more to life. This mortal coil is not all there is. And Jesus Christ came to set you free and give you an abundant life (John 10:10).

FILM TO FAITH

Watch one or both of these movies:

- *Man of Steel*
- *The Passion of the Christ* (mature audiences)

Ask:

- How did each hero show that he was both human and something else?
- How did the heroes relate to God?
- How did they live in the world but not of the world?
- What can you learn from each of them?
- How did each hero show selfless love for others?
- How have you resolved the tension between living in God's kingdom and in the world?

Father, I want to be the person you created and called me to be, and I want to live my life in your kingdom. Help me show the fruit of the Holy Spirit to every person, manifest the gifts of the Holy Spirit, and take every thought captive for you.

LOOKING AHEAD

Are you ever afraid or even just anxious? See the next devotion.

Remember!

The Ten Commandments (1956)
Gravity
Finding Dory

Are you ever afraid or even just anxious? How do you get over fear/anxiety?

Throughout the Bible, we are commanded to fear not. God tells us in Isaiah 41:10, "So do not fear, for I am with you; do not be dismayed, for I am your God. I will strengthen you and help you; I will uphold you with my righteous right hand." And Jesus encourages us in John 14:27, "Peace I leave with you; my peace I give you. I do not give to you as the world gives. Do not let your hearts be troubled and do not be afraid."

Sometimes, however, this is easier said than done. But another frequent command in the Bible will help: "Remember." Why should we remember? So that we're not afraid because we recall how God is always there for us. When we forget His presence and His intervention in our lives, we often become afraid of the problems, trials, and tribulations we face every day.

This advice was given to the Jews in Deuteronomy 5:15: "Remember that you were slaves in Egypt and that the LORD your God brought you out of there with a mighty hand and an outstretched arm." And it was pronounced in Deuteronomy 7:18, "But do not be afraid of them; remember well what the LORD your God did to Pharaoh and to all Egypt."

In fact, God tells the Israelites quite often throughout the Old Testament (and I paraphrase), "Look, you don't have to be afraid. I got rid of Pharaoh, I turned you from being slaves to being free men. I took you through the Red Sea. I brought you into the desert. I fed you manna, then I fed you quail."

Even so, do you remember what they did? They mumbled, grumbled, and whined. We often do the same thing.

Jesus emphasized the importance of remembering in Matthew 16:9: "Do you still not understand? Don't you remember the five loaves for the five thousand, and how many basketfuls you gathered?" Paul did too in Ephesians 2:12: "Remember that at that time you were separate from Christ, excluded from citizenship in Israel and foreigners to the covenants of the promise, without hope and without God in the world."

The quintessential movie to remember is Cecil B. DeMille's 1956 classic, *The Ten Commandments*, starring Charlton Heston and Yul Brynner. Many other movies depicting the story of Moses have also been produced, and in all of them, the people of Israel constantly forget the great miracles God has done and need to be reminded. They even whine about the food and ask to go back to slavery in Egypt. Sometimes they seem very modern.

In the movie *Gravity*, heroine Ryan Stone must remember the pain in her life to regain the will to pray to live. And in *Finding Dory*, a fish with short-term memory loss has to remember her home and her family to overcome her fears.

How do we get over being afraid? By looking at what God has done for us.

He's done mighty things in my life. I've already talked about my nefarious past. But that all ended when God saved me. The chain-smoking, the drugs, the philandering stopped without any desire to stop them. God rescued me. And then a week later, I got married to my beautiful wife, and a few years later I had my first son, and then I had two more sons and a beautiful daughter. I'm telling you, God does miraculous things.

So look back at your life. See what God's done to protect you and provide for you. Then you won't be afraid. And freed from fear, you can go forth in the power of His grace because you know that He is present in your life.

FILM TO FAITH

Watch one or more of these movies:

- *The Ten Commandments* (1956)
- *Gravity*
- *Finding Dory*

Ask:

- How was the hero or heroine afraid?
- What did they fear?
- How did they act when they were afraid?
- When and how did they remember?
- What difference did remembering make in their life?
- How have you triumphed over fear by remembering God's blessings in your life?
- What are God's blessings in your life?

Father, I do get anxious, worried, and even afraid of the future. Help me to remember your presence and provision in my life so I can live free from fear and anxiety and show everyone the victory you provide in Jesus Christ.

LOOKING AHEAD

Have you ever faced the impossible? See the next devotion.

Prayer and Fasting

MOVIES THAT INSPIRE
The 33 (mature audiences)
War Room

Have you ever faced the impossible?

One of the greatest miracles is portrayed in *The 33*, a movie based on the true story of thirty-three miners trapped 2,300 feet deep in a north Chilean mine in 2010. They're faced with only three days of food, practically no water, and a piece of rock the weight of two Empire State buildings sealing their exit and pressing down on their location for sixty-nine days.

One miner, Mario Sepúlveda (Antonio Banderas) extols them to fast and hope. Another of the men is an evangelical minister, José Henríquez (Marco Treviño), who prays in the name of Jesus, leads an alcoholic miner to Christ, and, along with Mario, gives the miners hope. On the day their food runs out, they have visions of the sacrament of communion.

While *The 33* shows the most extreme of circumstances, *War Room* portrays a more common but still often intractable and impossible problem—a marriage destroyed by selfishness, infidelity, and deception. A wonderful, wise, older woman named Clara (Karen Abercrombie) helps a disgusted and distraught wife, Elizabeth (Priscilla Shirer), learn the power of sacrifice and prayer to reunite with her husband, Tony (T.C. Stallings).

When faced with the incurable and impossible, Jesus said

that these problems and demons can only be cast out with praying and fasting. In Matthew 17, the disciples are asked to cure a boy with seizures, perhaps epilepsy, but they can't. "The disciples approached Jesus privately and said, 'Why couldn't we drive it out?' 'Because of your little faith,' He told them. 'For I assure you: If you have faith the size of a mustard seed, you will tell this mountain, 'Move from here to there,' and it will move. Nothing will be impossible for you. [However, this kind does not come out except by prayer and fasting]'" (Matthew 17:19–21 HCSB).

In 1990, Dr. Bill Bright called together many Christian leaders and asked them to fast and pray for the country for forty days. I thought to myself, *Fast? I'm a teddy bear. You think teddy bears want to fast? This is ridiculous. I enjoy food. I'm not gonna do this.* Then about a month later, my pastor called on all the congregation to fast and pray for forty days. This time I thought, *I don't want to do this, but this is getting too close for comfort.* Then I got an audiotape in the mail calling me to fast and pray for forty days.

So I fasted and prayed for forty days, and miracles happened. We produced a big event in Hollywood called the Annual Movieguide® Faith & Values Awards Gala and Report to the Entertainment Industry to encourage Hollywood leaders to produce more movies with faith and values. I didn't expect anyone to show up, but God filled the room with many Hollywood executives. The next year we did a bigger gala, so I started fasting and praying for forty days each year, and then I ate a lot during the rest of the year to make up for it!

What then happened was amazing (the incredible statistics are given at the beginning of this book, in "Glad to Have the Light: Of the Bible and the Screen"). God answered our prayers!

If you have an impossible problem, try what Jesus Christ suggested: fast and pray. You can cast out the demons of our age by fasting and praying in the name of Jesus.

FILM TO FAITH

Watch one or both of these movies:

- *The 33* (mature audiences)
- *War Room*

Ask:

- What was the impossible problem the hero or heroine was facing?
- How did they come to the decision to fast and pray?
- How did God move to solve the impossible problem?
- What has God done when you fasted and prayed?
- How have impossible problems been resolved in your life when you fasted and prayed?

Father, I am facing an impossible problem, (explain to God what your problem or situation is). Help me focus on you and your solution through fasting and prayer. I am weak, but you are strong. Help me fast and pray, and deliver me from my problem in Jesus Christ's name by the power of the Holy Spirit.

LOOKING AHEAD

Do you have a vision to do great things, but find yourself struggling against the world, the flesh, and the evil in your life? See the next devotion.

More Than Conquerors

MOVIES THAT INSPIRE
The Lord of the Rings: The Fellowship of the Ring
Mr. Smith Goes to Washington
World Trade Center

Do you have a vision to do great things, but find yourself struggling against the world, the flesh, and the evil in your life? Are you resigned to just get by or to even just survive? How would you live if you were more than a conqueror?

Romans 8:37 says, "No, in all these things we are more than conquerors through him who loved us." That's a tough concept. At least it was for me for many years, but here's an analogy that helps.

Famous boxer George Foreman's career had two phases. When he first went into the boxing ring, he won the heavyweight championship after several tough matches. However, when he lost a major fight, he became bitter. Then, in 1977, he almost died. So he prayed and dedicated his life to Jesus Christ. As a result, he started an inner-city youth center in Houston, Texas.

Now George didn't know how to raise money and hadn't figured out how to sell grills yet, so he couldn't keep the ministry going. In 1988, he decided to go back into the ring after ten years of retirement, and everybody said, "George, you're too old! You can't do this!" With limited resources, in 1994 at age forty-five, he regained a portion of the heavyweight championship. He donated most of the money to his inner-city youth ministry, and the youth there became "more than conquerors."

How are we more than conquerors? Through Jesus winning the victory on the cross. We don't have to fight that battle all over again; it has been won for us by Jesus, and when we get to heaven, we receive a crown.

In *The Lord of the Rings: The Fellowship of the Ring*, Frodo isn't a conventional or extraordinary hero. Rather, he's a short, unexceptional, humble Hobbit. He's chosen to take the inherently evil Ring through a hellish kingdom to be destroyed in the fires of Mount Doom, because he doesn't seek the power of the Ring. He's more than a conqueror because he's willing to carry the Ring.

Even at the climax, the unseen hand of Providence seems to determine that Frodo fails; however, in the end the hand of Providence intercedes to make sure the mission succeeds. Even so, Frodo can't be proud of his accomplishment. He is not the conqueror, because he only inherits the victory won by Providence through the defeat of another evil.

Director Frank Capra's 1939 masterpiece, *Mr. Smith Goes to Washington*, tells the story of a common man, Jefferson "Jeff" Smith, who's appointed to finish out the term of a senator who died while in office. The political bosses believe Jeff is a simpleton, a patsy. However, when Jeff realizes he's being used, the bosses try to frame him. He gets recognized to speak on the resolution calling for his expulsion, and he stages a filibuster where he speaks against corruption and reads from the Constitution and even the Bible.

Like Frodo, Jeff fails at his mission and collapses, but the battle is won because his inspired words have convicted the older mentor who had betrayed Jeff of his own sins. The battle isn't really won by Jeff; it's won by the Bible and the Constitution, and Jeff inherits the victory by recognizing in public these great chronicles of the real battle and the real victory.

In *World Trade Center*, a Marine in the reserves hears about the attack on the Twin Towers on September 11, 2001. When he prays at his church about the horrors of the aftermath of 9/11, he feels called to put on his Marine uniform and go to New York City to do something to help. Eventually, by the grace of God alone, he miraculously finds two Port Authority police officers, who have been praying and trusting God to be rescued, trapped deep in the rubble of the collapsed towers. The situation is impossible, but the officers are rescued by the victorious saving grace of God. They are more than conquerors because God Himself has won the victory *for* them.

Now that we have the victory in Christ, we can occupy. We can settle. We can grow. We can flourish. And that's what we've done with the Christian Film & Television Commission® ministry. When we started, there were only a few movies each year with positive Christian content, but now it's nearly 65 percent. When we started, there were only six family films, but now it's almost 40 percent.

By the way, the supreme victory is the one that Jesus Christ won over death itself. We are ultimately more than conquerors, because if we know Jesus Christ as our personal Lord and Savior, then we will triumph over death and live eternally with Him in heaven. So once we get that crown in heaven, we put it at His feet because we love Him so much and because He made us more than conquerors.

FILM TO FAITH

Watch one or more of these movies:

- *The Lord of the Rings: The Fellowship of the Ring*
- *Mr. Smith Goes to Washington*
- *World Trade Center*

Ask:

- How did God win the victory in each movie and make the hero more than a conqueror?
- How did the heroes turn to God?
- How were the heroes ordinary folks?
- How did Jesus Christ win the victory and make you more than a conqueror?
- What does it mean for you to be more than a conqueror?
- How should you then live as more than a conqueror?

Father, I am so grateful that Jesus Christ won the victory for me on the cross. Empower me to live my life in the light of His victory as more than a conqueror, freed from fear and anxiety.

LOOKING AHEAD

Are you caught in a rut? Has God put desires on your heart that aren't happening? See the next devotion.

Keep Your Eyes on Jesus
to Walk on Water

Son of God

Leap of Faith

Indiana Jones and the Last Crusade

Are you caught in a rut? Has God put desires on your heart that aren't happening?

The great news is that you can step out of the boat or the rut or the just-getting-by lifestyle to walk in faith.

In Matthew 14:24–33, Jesus calls Peter to walk in faith on the water:

> But the boat was already over a mile from land, battered by the waves, because the wind was against them. Around three in the morning, He came toward them walking on the sea. When the disciples saw Him walking on the sea, they were terrified. "It's a ghost!" they said, and cried out in fear. Immediately Jesus spoke to them. "Have courage! It is I. Don't be afraid." "Lord, if it's You," Peter answered Him, "command me to come to You on the water." "Come!" He said. And climbing out of the boat, Peter started walking on the water and came toward Jesus. But when he saw the strength of the wind, he was afraid. And beginning to sink, he cried out, "Lord, save me!" Immediately Jesus reached

out His hand, caught hold of him, and said to him, "You of little faith, why did you doubt?" When they got into the boat, the wind ceased. Then those in the boat worshiped Him and said, "Truly You are the Son of God!" (HCSB)

Interestingly, there have been more than 150 movies made about Jesus since 1897, but few include His walking on the water. *Son of God* does show this powerful, supernatural event in the midst of a storm. The point is that Peter must keep his eyes on Jesus Christ, and so must you and I.

Many movies have scenes where the hero or heroine must take a leap of faith and metaphorically walk on water. One example is the movie by that name, *Leap of Faith*. It's about a fake faith healer named Jonas Nightengale (Steve Martin), who's confronted by a real healing when the young boy Boyd comes on stage, clutches the feet of the statue of Jesus on the cross, and miraculously walks for the first time and throws away his crutches. Jonas realizes God is real and leaves behind his life of taking advantage of people. It is Boyd who keeps his eyes on Jesus Christ and walks.

Indiana Jones and the Last Crusade has clear Christian symbols and references. Indy (Harrison Ford) must find the Holy Grail to save his wounded father, but to do this, he must pass three traps that serve as spiritual tests. At the first, he must kneel in repentance to avoid being decapitated. At the second, he must step on cobblestones to spell out the Old Testament name for God, Jehovah. And at the third test, he must literally take a leap of faith.

I once had a friend whom I'd visit every year. He was making a good salary and had two children and a wonderful wife. When he told me, "I want to be in the entertainment industry," I said, "If God has called you, then you have to step out of the boat." I repeated that to him two years in a row.

Finally, he left his job and couldn't get another one. I thought, *Oh no. I've caused him to do something drastic and he's sinking.* However, as soon as he put his eyes on Jesus (which was very soon), he got a terrific job. He was able to be in the entertainment industry and do all the things he wanted to do, and he was making more money than he did in his previous job.

Now that's not always the way it's going to happen, but things will work out when you keep your eyes on Jesus. You can walk on water in the world as you take every thought captive for Christ.

FILM TO FAITH

Watch one or all of these movies:

- *Son of God*
- *Leap of Faith* (mature audiences)
- *Indiana Jones and the Last Crusade*

Ask:

- Why did Jesus ask Peter to walk on the water in the storm?
- What was the reaction of the disciples when Peter walked on water?
- Why did Jonas refuse to take a leap of faith, while Boyd took it?
- How did Indiana Jones have the courage to take a leap of faith?
- What are the desires that God has placed on your heart (not your wishes and whims)?
- How are you pursuing the plans God has for you?
- How can you get out of a rut and walk with Jesus to do mighty deeds for Him?

Father, I want to get out of the safety of the boat and walk with you on the water to do the wonderful deeds you have called me to do. Help me follow you wherever you lead, to proclaim the good news of your kingdom come in word and deed.

LOOKING AHEAD

Have you forgotten the encouraging words that God speaks to you? See the next devotion.

Man's or God's
Point of View

Extremely Loud and Incredibly Close
Risen

Have you forgotten the encouraging words that God speaks to you?

We can look at Scripture in terms of two big words: theocentric (God's point of view) or anthropocentric (our point of view). It's either His way or what we think is our way.

Hebrews 12:5–6 presents God's point of view: "Have you forgotten the encouraging words which God speaks to you as his children? 'My child, pay attention when the Lord corrects you, and do not be discouraged when he rebukes you. Because the Lord corrects everyone he loves, and punishes everyone he accepts as a child'" (GNT). How do we see that demonstrated in our lives?

When my second son was a little boy, he used to purposely kick a ball across a busy street where our dog had been hit by a truck. I'd say, "No," but he'd kick the ball again. I'd say, "Jim, don't do that," and he'd kick the ball again. Finally, I had to discipline him, and he looked at me and said, "I hate you."

Now, he's a major in the Marine Corps and an attorney at the US Attorney's office in New Orleans. We are very close. I was willing to love him, even when it meant telling him not to do something that he thought defined his freedom.

Have you ever felt that you were pursuing your rights but it wasn't in your best interest? Or maybe you thought it was in your best interest, but God said, "No. There's a better way. There's a more beautiful way. There's a way that's going to free you."

In the excellent movie *Extremely Loud and Incredibly Close*, nine-year-old Oskar (Thomas Horn) and his dad are very close. Oskar has been tested for Asperger syndrome, but the results were inconclusive. On "the worst day," as Oskar calls 9/11, he's sent home early from school and hears messages on the home phone from his father, who's in a meeting in one of the two World Trade Center towers. Oskar can't pick up the phone when the sixth call comes. It's clear from this message that his father thinks Oskar is there and just wants to tell him how much he loves him.

Oskar hides the message machine in the closet so his mother doesn't know about the messages. There he finds a key in a manila envelope with the name *Black* on it, and he thinks the key is a clue his father left for him that will explain everything. Oskar decides to search New York for everyone with the name Black to find out what the key unlocks.

One of the people he visits is holding a church service in her home, and they pray for Oskar in the name of Jesus. Oskar says he doesn't believe, but the woman tells him that if he finds the answer to the key, it's a miracle. The rest of the movie fulfills her prophecy.

From Oskar's point of view, the world has fallen apart. From God's point of view, Oskar is discovering that God loves him. God's love answers Oskar's questions and heals his family.

Risen tells the story of a superior Roman military tribune, Clavius, who hunts for Jesus Christ's body, not realizing Jesus has risen from the dead. Clavius makes sure the Roman soldiers crucified Jesus in the correct manner, but when he sends some soldiers to the tomb, they fall asleep on the job, and Christ's body is not in the tomb. Now Clavius must find Jesus' body.

When they go to Mary Magdalene, she tells them they can't find Jesus' body because He's risen from the dead. More followers then go to Clavius with the same story, and he wonders if this could be true.

From Clavius' point of view, life is constant killing in the name of the power of Rome. From Jesus' point of view, Clavius will find a day without death in the reality of His resurrection. Slowly, Clavius becomes aware of the truth that life is more than his point of view.

The good news is that God sometimes puts a bit of a roadblock in front of us so that we find true freedom, which is to be the person that He has designed us to be. So instead of looking at life from your point of view, look at it from God's point of view.

The best place to find God's point of view is the Bible. It will help you get perspective on the good news in your life.

FILM TO FAITH

Watch one or both of these movies:

- *Extremely Loud and Incredibly Close*
- *Risen*

Ask:

- What was the hero's point of view?
- How did the hero discover God's point of view?
- What difference did it make in the hero's life to discover God's point of view?
- When have you discovered God's point of view?

o   When you discovered God's point of view, how did it change you?

Father, sometimes I seem to be struggling against every-thing. Sometimes my life seems so hard. Pour out your Holy Spirit on me to help me understand your Word, the Bible, so I am able to live at peace knowing that you are in charge of my life.

LOOKING AHEAD

Do you need the power and freedom of God's grace? See the next devotion.

10

The Power of Grace

MOVIES THAT INSPIRE
A Christmas Carol (1999)
The Preacher's Wife

Do you need the power of God's grace? Do you need the freedom of His grace?

In Section Five of John Bunyan's classic book *The Pilgrim's Progress*, as pilgrims Faithful and Christian are walking to the Celestial City, another pilgrim comes along. They call him Talkative because, of course, he talks a lot. He has all the right answers from Scripture and knows everything that's happening on the road to the Celestial City. Rather than let Talkative come with them, Christian suggests to Faithful, "Why, go to him, and enter into some serious discourse about the power of religion; and ask him plainly (when he has approved of it, for that he will) whether this thing be set up in his heart, house, or conversation."

When Faithful asks Talkative about the power of grace, he equivocates. He can't quite nail it, because the power of grace is to be transformed and thus to abhor sin. As Christian says:

Remember the proverb, They say, and do not; but the kingdom of God is not in word, but in power. He talketh of prayer, of repentance, of faith, and of the new birth; but he knows but only to talk of them. I have been in his family, and have observed him both at home and abroad; and I know what I say of him is the truth. His house is as empty of religion, as the white of an egg is of savour. There is neither prayer, nor sign of repentance for sin: yea, the brewer, in his kind, serves God far better than he.[3]

Christian in *The Pilgrim's Progress* points us to 2 Corinthians 9:8, which says, "And God is able to make every grace overflow to you, so that in every way, always having everything you need, you may excel in every good work," and to Romans 6:14, which says, "For sin will not rule over you, because you are not under law but under grace" (HCSB).

Once you know the power of grace, you are free to be yourself, to do what God has designed you to do: to be happy, to give thanks, and to pray constantly. This is very good news.

The 1999 TV version of *A Christmas Carol* is a Christian version with a great church scene that recaptures the essence of the power of God's grace. Scrooge is well-versed in the Christian religion. When he's confronted by the visions of Christmas past, Christmas present, and Christmas future, the Holy Spirit convicts Scrooge, and he goes to church repentant and transformed.

In *The Preacher's Wife*, Henry Biggs (Courtney B. Vance), the pastor of a run-down, inner-city church, is burned out. Henry's given everything he has in service to God, and the last straw is that a greedy developer, Joe Hamilton (Gregory Hines), has bought the mortgage on the church and wants to turn it into a mall. In desperation, Henry utters one last prayer to God. Suddenly, the angel Dudley (Denzel Washington) falls out of heaven. Henry has to move beyond knowing about Christianity to exhibit the power of grace and real love.

So it's not how strong you are. It's not how much faith you have.

---

3 John Bunyan, *The Pilgrim's Progress from This World to That Which Is to Come*, C. J. Lovik, ed. (Wheaton: Crossway, 2009), 38–39.

It's how strong God is. God is strong enough to give you the power of His grace to transcend the temptations, trials, and tribulations of this world, and to go into all the world to be His minister and witness.

FILM TO FAITH

Watch one or both of these movies:

- *The Christmas Carol* (1999)
- *The Preacher's Wife*

Ask:

- How did the hero go from knowing about Christianity to knowing the power of God's love and grace?
- What difference did it make in the hero's life when he was transformed by the power of God's grace?
- How have you been transformed by the power of God's grace?
- What difference does that transformation make in your life?

Father, I know there is much more to the Christian life than just knowing about Christianity. Empower me by your grace to manifest your Word in my life in such a powerful way that people want to know you when they meet me.

LOOKING AHEAD

Do you experience joy when you celebrate Christmas? See the next devotion.

11

He Makes Us Glad

MOVIES THAT INSPIRE
The Purple Rose of Cairo
A Charlie Brown Christmas

Do you experience joy when you celebrate Christmas?

The December 25 reading from *The Book of Common Prayer* includes, "O God, you make us glad by the yearly festival of the birth of your only Son Jesus Christ." However, many people get depressed at Christmas.

In one of the best television short movies ever made, *A Charlie Brown Christmas*, Charlie Brown is depressed by the commercialization of Christmas. He tries to direct a Christmas play, but his efforts are mocked. Then Linus tells Charlie Brown the true meaning of Christmas, and Charlie Brown cheers up to celebrate the Christmas season with his friends.

Like a great movie script, the Bible tells you where it is going and then tells you the story. Isaiah 9:2, 6–7 looks forward to the story of salvation:

> The people who walked in darkness have seen a great light; those who lived in a land of deep darkness—on them light has shined. … For a child has been born for us, a son given to us; authority rests upon his shoulders; and he is named Wonderful Counselor, Mighty God, Everlasting Father, Prince of Peace. His authority shall grow continually, and there shall be endless peace for the throne of David and

his kingdom. He will establish and uphold it with justice and with righteousness from this time onward and forevermore. The zeal of the LORD of hosts will do this. (NRSV)

The gladness that Isaiah predicts was the birth of the child, which came after hundreds of years of the fervent prayers of his people. This child was a Wonderful Counselor, the Prince of Peace, and our Everlasting Father, an insight to the truth of the Trinity. Our salvation will come from one who is God the Father, Jesus our Lord, and the Holy Spirit—all in one.

An imperfect but helpful analogy about the one substance of each member of the Trinity is the Woody Allen movie *The Purple Rose of Cairo*. In it, Cecilia (Mia Farrow), is watching a movie with the same title, *The Purple Rose of Cairo*, in the midst of the Great Depression. After Cecilia watches the movie over and over, the hero in the movie, Tom Baxter (Jeff Daniels), looks at her and steps out of the screen and into her life. Movies all over the world stop, and the filmmakers send the actor who played the hero to get the hero character to go back into the movie.

Eventually, the actor and the hero meet in a church and wrestle under a large crucifix. Of course, the actor and the hero are one substance. If the writer were the director who also played the hero, then the analogy would be established.

Luke tells why the birth of Jesus makes us glad in Luke 2:8–20:

In that region, there were shepherds living in the fields, keeping watch over their flock by night. Then an angel of the Lord stood before them, and the glory of the Lord shone around them, and they were terrified. But the angel said to them, "Do not be afraid; for see—I am bringing you good news of great joy for all the people: to you is born this day in the city of David a Savior, who is the

Messiah, the Lord. This will be a sign for you: you will find a child wrapped in bands of cloth and lying in a manger." And suddenly there was with the angel a multitude of the heavenly host, praising God and saying, "Glory to God in the highest heaven, and on earth peace among those whom he favors!" When the angels had left them and gone into heaven, the shepherds said to one another, "Let us go now to Bethlehem and see this thing that has taken place, which the Lord has made known to us." So, they went with haste and found Mary and Joseph, and the child lying in the manger. When they saw this, they made known what had been told them about this child; and all who heard it were amazed at what the shepherds told them. But Mary treasured all these words and pondered them in her heart. The shepherds returned, glorifying and praising God for all they had heard and seen, as it had been told them. (NRSV)

Luke's history makes us glad that the real emperor of the universe, Jesus Christ, came humbly as a loving baby, rather than as a cruel Caesar. We are glad that Jesus is a gift to people like the shepherds, the lowliest of the low. We are glad that He came to set us free. And it makes us very glad that we have a new birth, a new Father, a new family, a new name, a new hope, and a new home in heaven.

FILM TO FAITH

Watch one or both of these movies:

- *A Charlie Brown Christmas*
- *The Purple Rose of Cairo*

Ask:

- How does Charlie Brown discover the good news of Christmas?
- What makes Charlie Brown glad?
- How does *The Purple Rose of Cairo* serve as a flawed analogy about the one substance of the Trinity?
- How and why does Christmas make you glad?

Father, whenever I am overwhelmed by the hustle and bustle of Christmas, or even just the hectic nature of life, help me to understand the breadth, depth, and magnificence of your birth, sacrifice, and resurrection, so that I am filled with the joy that comes from giving you thanks. Please make me glad by the power of the Holy Spirit, in the name of Jesus Christ.

LOOKING AHEAD

Have you experienced pain, suffering, and need? See the next devotion.

12

God's Tender Love for You and Me

Ben-Hur
The Elephant Man

Have you experienced pain, suffering, and need? Do you want God to love and care for you?

In *The Elephant Man*, John Merrick (John Hurt), who is modeled after the real Joseph Merrick, is a severely deformed British man who was exhibited as a freak by Mr. Bytes (Freddie Jones). John's life is a painful horror, physically and psychologically. When Dr. Treves (Anthony Hopkins) examines John, he discovers that John is quite intelligent and a Christian (John recites the Twenty-third Psalm). John's life was filled with pain and suffering, yet he found God's love even as he lived his own painful passion of deformity and alienation.

Judah Ben-Hur (Charlton Heston), in the 1959 movie *Ben-Hur*, is a Jewish prince who is betrayed and sent into slavery by a Roman friend, Messala (Stephen Boyd). After years of pain, suffering, and need, he discovers God's tender love when he meets Jesus Christ in the midst of his passion.

Jesus Christ's passion is the story of love and redemption, where the violence against Jesus assures us of God's tender mercy. This is the Jesus described in John 1:1–3: "In the beginning was the Word, and the Word was with God, and the Word was God. He was with God in the beginning. All things were created through Him, and apart from Him not one thing was created that has been created" (HCSB).

This Creator of the universe became fully man and fully God so He could take upon Himself our sins to give us the ultimate victory, which was made manifest by His resurrection.

The words of Matthew 27:45, 50–54 are incredible:

> From noon on, darkness came over the whole land until three in the afternoon. … Then Jesus cried again with a loud voice and breathed his last. At that moment, the curtain of the temple was torn in two, from top to bottom. The earth shook, and the rocks were split. The tombs also were opened, and many bodies of the saints who had fallen asleep were raised. After his resurrection, they came out of the tombs and entered the holy city and appeared to many. Now, when the centurion and those with him, who were keeping watch over Jesus, saw the earthquake and what took place, they were terrified and said, "Truly this man was God's Son!" (NRSV)

Jesus died at three o'clock in the afternoon, the time of the evening sacrifice. That is the time of the sin offering. And where were those lambs for the sin offering born? In Bethlehem, close to Jerusalem. The purest lamb was taken and sacrificed and died at three o'clock. But this time, the sinless lamb was Jesus Christ, the ultimate sacrifice.

At that moment, the curtain of the temple was torn from top to bottom. The curtain was as thick as the palm of your hand, thirty feet high and sixty feet long. It took three hundred people to put it up on the hooks because it was so heavy.

The high priest and all the rest of the religious rulers were shaken. Why? Because suddenly everyone had access to God. The barrier to entry had been removed. Then the tombs opened, and the bodies of many saints were raised and came out of the tombs and entered the holy city to be seen by many people.

All these resurrections, including that of Lazarus, are telling us that Jesus Christ's resurrection is not just about Jesus; it's about us. It's about each of us who will be resurrected.

In the early church, up until the time of Constantine, all the paintings were of the resurrected Jesus. Today, if you go to Ravenna, Italy, you see the resurrected Jesus in the mosaic art of the older churches. If you go up to Galilee, you'll see the resurrected Jesus in the mosaics. The crucified Jesus was featured only after Emperor Constantine saw the cross in the air, and God told him to paint the cross on his standards and that became the focal point. But the story didn't end with Jesus dying on the cross; it ends with Jesus Christ's resurrection.

God loves us so much that He gave His only begotten Son, Jesus Christ, to save you and me. This is God's terrible but tender love for us.

What God is calling you to do today is to believe. He wants you to believe, receive healing, receive forgiveness, receive new life, and be resurrected to spend eternity with Him. That belief is a gift from God. So believe in Jesus Christ, receive God's tender love, and become an adopted child of God and heir of His eternal glory.

FILM TO FAITH

Watch one or both of these movies:

- *Ben-Hur* (1959)
- *The Elephant Man*

Ask:

- How do these movies show the pain, suffering, and needs of the hero?
- How do these movies show God's tender love?
- How has God's tender love overcome the pain, suffering, and need in your life?
- How has God loved and cared for you?

Father, life is full of pain, suffering, and need, and I need you, Jesus, and your tender love to give me the victory of your resurrection. Father, hear my prayers by the power of the name of Jesus Christ.

LOOKING AHEAD

Do you want life and prosperity, or death and adversity? See the next devotion.

13

Choose This Day

MOVIES THAT INSPIRE

Grace Unplugged

Schindler's List (mature audiences)

Do you want life and prosperity, or death and adversity?

Given the choice, who would choose death and adversity? Yet we know that people choose death every single day. They choose self-destructive behavior. They choose to be cruel. From the Romans to the Nazis to ISIS, there are too many who choose death.

What about those of us who want life and prosperity? Is it as simple as Deuteronomy 30:15–20:

> See, I have set before you today life and prosperity, death and adversity. If you obey the commandments of the LORD your God that I am commanding you today, by loving the LORD your God, walking in his ways, and observing his commandments, decrees, and ordinances, then you shall live and become numerous, and the LORD your God will bless you in the land that you are entering to possess. But if your heart turns away and you do not hear, but are led astray to bow down to other gods and serve them, I declare to you today that you shall perish; you shall not live long in the land that you are crossing the Jordan to enter and possess. I call heaven and earth to witness against you today that I have set before you life and death, blessings and curses. Choose life so that you and your descendants may

live, loving the LORD your God, obeying him, and holding fast to him; for that means life to you and length of days, so that you may live in the land that the LORD swore to give to your ancestors, to Abraham, to Isaac, and to Jacob. (NRSV)

In this passage, choosing life is a wonderful, slow-maturing process, like in agriculture. We plant in the spring and harvest in the fall. It's not instant pudding. When we plant in the spring and harvest in the fall, a lot of things can happen. There are days that are burning hot and we think, *I'm never going to get a harvest.* And there are the days when the hurricane comes and we think, *I'm never going to get a harvest.*

Sometimes the harvest is in eternity. Often, the ultimate harvest is generational. That is long-term thinking. Sometimes people choose death and adversity because they want instant gratification. They can't wait. We have to wait for the blessings of God.

God says in that Deuteronomy passage that His promises are for our benefit. Heaven and earth are witnesses to those promises. They may not be instant promises, but they're promises that He's given us.

In *Schindler's List*, Oskar Schindler (Liam Neeson) is a German Nazi war profiteer. He has chosen to prosper by paying bribes and using the cheap labor of the Jews whom the Nazis have impoverished. However, as he gets to know the Jews, especially his Jewish manager, Itzhak Stern (Ben Kingsley), and as he sees the vile treatment of the Jews by the Nazi SS, he begins to choose life, eventually saving twelve hundred Jews but losing all his money. He chooses life but only prospers vicariously through the "Schindler Jews" who survive and their descendants.

In that light, it's interesting to note the last scene, when Oskar laments to his Jewish friends that he could have saved more Jews if only he had sold more of his possessions, especially the gold swastika pin he owns. Moved by Oskar's tearful, heartfelt statement of regret, the Jews surround and comfort him. In this way, *Schindler's List* shows us that we can never do enough to achieve real peace and salvation. As Ephesians 2:8–10 says, "For it is by grace you have been saved, through faith—and this is not from yourselves, it is the gift of God—not by works, so that no one can boast. For we are God's handiwork, created in Christ Jesus to do good works, which God prepared in advance for us to do."

A choice that is faced more often by contemporary young people is Gracie Trey's choice in *Grace Unplugged*. Gracie has been raised by her mother and her father, a successful musician who gave up his career when Jesus Christ came into his life. Gracie chooses to run away to Hollywood to become a famous musician. When she starts to see through the false glitter of Tinseltown, she chooses life and goes back home. Slowly, her life is blessed. Two years later, she's invited to sing at a major concert and gets engaged.

What do we do when we make the choice between being joyous and satisfied, or being unsatisfied, angry, selfish? When we make the choice for life, for long-term living, for compassion, we make the choice for tomorrow.

God says that when you choose life, the Lord brings increase in your life—in your children, in your grandchildren, in the people you know, and in all the work you're doing.

So choose life and abundance, and boast of God's mercy and grace.

FILM TO FAITH

Watch one or both of these movies:

- *Grace Unplugged*
- *Schindler's List* (extreme caution recommended for wartime violence, nudity, and other mature content)

Ask:

- How does Oskar Schindler choose life and prosperity when he loses everything by saving the lives of the Jews?
- How does Gracie choose life and prosperity when she gives up the rich-and-famous music contract?
- What does God mean by life and prosperity?
- What do most people mean by life and prosperity?
- Why did you or would you want to choose God's promise of life and prosperity?

Father, the world beckons with promises of life and prosperity, but I want the real life and prosperity that only you can give me. Provide the discernment and wisdom to choose life and prosperity as you promise, not as the world promises.

LOOKING AHEAD

By what authority? See the next devotion.

By What Authority?

Evelyn

Hacksaw Ridge (mature audiences)

"By what authority?" is a foundational question. By what authority does some organization record your phone call with them—or demand you do something?

A brilliant Christian trademark attorney asked the fire inspector who came to inspect his new offices, "By what authority are you inspecting my offices?" Fire department superiors had to admit they had no authority under the state constitution to perform inspections, so they left the lawyer alone thereafter.

The issue of "by what authority" also gave the legal basis for the American Revolution. Samuel Rutherford in his book *Lex, Rex, or the Law and the Prince* (1644) argued from a biblical perspective that God's law was above the king, not the opposite. So just like any citizen, the king could not break God's law by stealing, lying, and murdering. In contrast, tyrants from Nebuchadnezzar to Hitler to Stalin insisted they had the authority to do whatever evil they wanted, including mass murder.

The movie *Evelyn* is based on a true story about a little girl seized by officials in Ireland in the early 1950s because her mother abandoned her father and her siblings to run away with another man. Evelyn's father, Desmond (Niall Beagen), fights for the custody of Evelyn (Sophie Vavasseur) all the way to the Irish Supreme

Court on the grounds that the Irish Constitution gives the father, not the state, the authority over his own children. Evelyn's prayers and faith in God are heartwarming.

In *Hacksaw Ridge*, Desmond Doss (Andrew Garfield) enlists in the army during World War II to serve as a non-combatant medic. He is a deeply religious Christian who refuses to touch a gun. His superior officers try to court-martial him, but his father gets a top commanding officer to write a letter stating that Desmond's pacifism is protected by an Act of Congress, and the officers have no authority to force him to carry a gun and violate his beliefs.

This question of authority comes up often in the Bible. Jesus tells Pilate that he only has the authority to try Jesus because that authority has been given to Pilate by God: "Pilate therefore said to him, 'Do you refuse to speak to me? Do you not know that I have power to release you, and power to crucify you?' Jesus answered him, 'You would have no power over me unless it had been given you from above; therefore, the one who handed me over to you is guilty of a greater sin'" John 19:10–11 (NRSV).

A very important question of "by what authority" also arises in Matthew 21:1–9:

When Jesus and his disciples had come near Jerusalem and had reached Bethphage, at the Mount of Olives, Jesus sent two disciples, saying to them, "Go into the village ahead of you, and immediately you will find a donkey tied, and a colt with her; untie them and bring them to me. If anyone says anything to you, just say this, 'The Lord needs them.' And he will send them immediately." This took place to fulfill what had been spoken through the prophet, saying, "Tell the daughter of Zion, Look, your king is coming to you, humble, and mounted on a donkey, and on a colt, the foal of a donkey." The disciples went and did as Jesus had directed them; they brought the donkey and the colt, and put their cloaks on them, and he sat on them. A very large crowd spread their cloaks on the road, and others cut branches from the trees and spread them on the road. The crowds that went ahead of him and that followed were shouting, "Hosanna to the Son of David! Blessed is the one who comes in the name of the Lord! Hosanna in the highest heaven!" (NRSV)

Jesus is fulfilling Old Testament prophecy every step of the way. Now imagine taking someone's car and telling them, "The Lord needs it!" This isn't going to work in twenty-first-century America, but it worked at the time of Jesus Christ because many people knew Jesus was fulfilling the Messianic prophesy.

People were yelling, "Hosanna," which is a very unique word in that it's a combination of a Hebrew word and an Aramaic word. One of them says, "Save us now" or "Heal us now, Lord," while the other says, "Blessed is he who comes in the name of the Lord."

The Pharisees were so upset that they told Jesus to tell the people to stop, but Jesus pointed out that God had ordained this outpouring of praise, and the Pharisees had no authority to stop it: "Some of the Pharisees in the crowd said to him, 'Teacher, order your disciples to stop.' He answered, 'I tell you, if these were silent, the stones would shout out'" (Luke 19:39–40 NRSV).

You have been commanded and have the authority from God to witness for Jesus, and the world does not have the authority to stop you. The world can resort to force, but Jesus Christ is the authority and has called you to go into all the world to proclaim the kingdom of God.

FILM TO FAITH

Watch one or both of these movies:

- *Evelyn*
- *Hacksaw Ridge* (mature audiences)

Ask:

- How did each movie reveal the difference between legitimate authority and illegitimate authority?
- How was God revealed as the source for legitimate authority?
- How do you know what is legitimate authority or illegitimate authority?
- Why is understanding legitimate authority important?

Father, there are many people, organizations, and political institutions claiming authority in my life. Help me to recognize your true authority so I have the wisdom to do what's right and avoid what's wrong.

LOOKING AHEAD

Have you obeyed God only to find yourself in dire need? See the next devotion.

The Lord Will Provide

MOVIES THAT INSPIRE

The Pursuit of Happyness
Miracles from Heaven

Have you obeyed God only to find yourself in dire need? Have you ever been at the end of your rope? How can that happen when the Bible tells us that the Lord will provide?

Genesis 22:1–14 is about radical faith and radical provision:

> God tested Abraham. He said to him, "Abraham!" And he said, "Here I am." He said, "Take your son, your only son Isaac, whom you love, and go to the land of Moriah, and offer him there as a burnt offering on one of the mountains that I shall show you." So Abraham rose early in the morning, saddled his donkey, and took two of his young men with him, and his son Isaac; he cut the wood for the burnt offering, and set out and went to the place in the distance that God had shown him. On the third day Abraham looked up and saw the place far away. Then Abraham said to his young men, "Stay here with the donkey; the boy and I will go over there; we will worship, and then we will come back to you." Abraham took the wood of the burnt offering and laid it on his son Isaac, and he himself carried the fire and the knife. So, the two of them walked on together. Isaac said to his father Abraham, "Father!" And he said, "Here I am, my son." He said, "The fire and the wood are here,

but where is the lamb for a burnt offering?" Abraham said, "God himself will provide the lamb for a burnt offering, my son." So the two of them walked on together. When they came to the place that God had shown him, Abraham built an altar there and laid the wood in order. He bound his son Isaac, and laid him on the altar, on top of the wood. Then Abraham reached out his hand and took the knife to kill his son. But the angel of the LORD called to him from heaven, and said, "Abraham, Abraham!" And he said, "Here I am." He said, "Do not lay your hand on the boy or do anything to him; for now I know that you fear God, since you have not withheld your son, your only son, from me." And Abraham looked up and saw a ram, caught in a thicket by its horns. Abraham went and took the ram and offered it up as a burnt offering instead of his son. So, Abraham called that place "The LORD will provide"; as it is said to this day, "On the mount of the LORD it shall be provided." (NRSV)

God tested Abraham to refine him. Isaac was the only son of the promise to Abraham that he would be the father of many nations. Now God calls him to take Isaac to Mount Moriah to offer Isaac as an offering. Abraham left his men at the mountain, telling them, "We will come back to you." He believed that both he and Isaac would return because God would give Isaac back to him.

In *The Pursuit of Happyness*, based on a true story, Chris Gardner (Will Smith) pursues the American Dream, but he loses his savings in the process. A chance meeting inspires him to take a stressful internship at a stock brokerage, but his personal life crumbles. His wife leaves him and their young son. Soon, Chris and his son are sleeping in shelters and a public restroom. God provides at the last moment, and miracles happen.

Miracles from Heaven is the true story of three years in the life of a very ill, ten-to-twelve-year-old Texan girl named Anna (Kylie Rogers). Anna's mother, Christy (Jennifer Garner), prays and seeks a cure for Anna. The doctors can't diagnose the problem, and the specialist in Boston has no time for Anna. God provides an opening in Dr. Nurko's schedule, but things get worse. Even so, Anna witnesses to her roommate who's dying of cancer. Anna convinces Dr. Nurko (Eugenio Derbez) that she must go home, and there, trying to play with her sisters, she falls into the hollow of a dead tree, sixty feet down. The firemen pull her out, everyone prays, and God provides a miracle.

Chris quietly trusted in God, and Christy and Anna trusted with passion and prayer. God provided. God loves you and will provide what you need.

FILM TO FAITH

Watch one or both of these movies:

- *The Pursuit of Happyness*
- *Miracles from Heaven*

Ask:

- How did God provide in *The Pursuit of Happyness* and *Miracles from Heaven*?
- How did Chris, Christy, and Anna reach out to God?
- How has God provided for you when you were at the end of your rope?

Father, Genesis 22 is a tough passage because Abraham knew he had to go to Moriah to sacrifice his only son. But he wasn't providing the sacrifice; you were. You've always provided the sacrifice. Let us not get ahead of you. Let us live in the Spirit of God and trust you to provide for all our needs as we fulfill the desires you've laid on our hearts. In Jesus' name, amen.

LOOKING AHEAD

Where do we find a good leader—a good shepherd? See the next devotion.

16

How to Find a Good Leader

MOVIES THAT INSPIRE
Shaun the Sheep
Quo Vadis

Where do we find a good leader—a good shepherd?

In the animated movie *Shaun the Sheep*, Shaun and the sheep want a day off, so they coax the shepherd into falling asleep in a small trailer. The trailer rolls down to the town, the shepherd bumps his head, and the tumble causes amnesia. Soon, the sheep realize they need a shepherd and search for him. They learn that even though they want to do their own thing, their shepherd's way is better.

Psalm 23 explains:

The LORD is my shepherd;
I shall not want.
He makes me to lie down in green pastures;
He leads me beside the still waters.
He restores my soul;
He leads me in the paths of righteousness
For His name's sake.
Yea, though I walk through the valley of the shadow of
    death,
I will fear no evil;

For You are with me;
Your rod and Your staff, they comfort me.
You prepare a table before me in the presence of my
    enemies;
You anoint my head with oil;
My cup runs over.
Surely goodness and mercy shall follow me
All the days of my life;
And I will dwell in the house of the LORD Forever. (NKJV)

Before he was chosen by God, David shepherded flocks of sheep in the mountains. He had to worry about lions and thieves. He tells us that by following the Good Shepherd, we "shall not want." Other "shepherds" promise that we shall not want, but then tax us to provide for us what they think we should want.

The Good Shepherd feeds us in green pastures and gives us wonderful rest in those green pastures, which are not easy to find. He refreshes us beside still waters. Sheep can't be watered at a waterfall or in a rushing stream, so he takes us to pools of safe water. He revives our soul. Some other translations say "He restores" our soul. Either way, when trials and tribulations are wearing away at us, this is great news. He guides us in the right paths to lead us to a more blessed life, and even through death itself, into the kingdom of God. His rod and his staff comfort us and protect us.

When two of my children, Robby and Evy, were little, we were skiing at Zermatt on the Matterhorn. While we were on the mountain, the resort closed the slope because of a storm. We couldn't see, and there were dangerous crevasses, so I put my ski pole out behind me like a staff to comfort and keep Robby and Evy in line to slowly ski down, praying all the way.

In the kingdom of God, Jesus invites us to the heavenly banquet, foreshadowed on earth by the Last Supper and communion, which was when He told us that He fulfilled all the promises in the Old Testament. We banquet in the presence of our enemies, who may be like the rich man who looked up from hell, saw Lazarus with Abraham, and begged, "Please, warn my brothers" (see Luke 16:14–23). Then He anoints us, healing us. He fills our cup to overflowing, which is amazing. Goodness and mercy shall follow us all the days of our life, and He shelters us forever.

In the great 1951 movie *Quo Vadis*, General Marcus (Robert Taylor) returns to Rome and falls in love with a Christian, Lygia (Deborah Kerr). Nero (Peter Ustinov) is persecuting the Christians. Peter (Finlay Currie) flees crucifixion, but outside the city meets the risen Jesus. In Latin, Peter asks Jesus, "*Quo vadis?*" or "Where are you going?" Jesus replies in Latin, "I am going to Rome to be crucified again." Before Peter is martyred, he follows Jesus' direction back to Rome to encourage Marcus and others to follow the Good Shepherd.

In John 10:1–10, Jesus explains:

> "Very truly, I tell you, anyone who does not enter the sheepfold by the gate but climbs in by another way is a thief and a bandit. The one who enters by the gate is the shepherd of the sheep. The gatekeeper opens the gate for him, and the sheep hear his voice. He calls his own sheep by name and leads them out. When he has brought out all his own, he goes ahead of them, and the sheep follow him because they know his voice. They will not follow a stranger, but they will run from him because they do not know the voice of strangers." Jesus used this figure of speech with them, but they did not understand what he was saying to them. So

again Jesus said to them, "Very truly, I tell you, I am the gate for the sheep. All who came before me are thieves and bandits; but the sheep did not listen to them. I am the gate. Whoever enters by me will be saved, and will come in and go out and find pasture. The thief comes only to steal and kill and destroy. I came that they may have life, and have it abundantly." (NRSV)

In the mountains, shepherds arrange a rock wall to keep out lions and thieves and then lie down, becoming the gate to protect the sheep. My daughter has also raised sheep. When flocks are mixed together, you call and your sheep come to you. The goats don't pay attention, but the sheep wisely recognize the voice of their shepherd.

Have you heard Jesus calling you? He gives you life more abundantly, so goodness and mercy will follow you forever. Follow Jesus, the Good Shepherd.

FILM TO FAITH

Watch one or both of these movies:

- *Shaun the Sheep*
- *Quo Vadis*

Ask:

- How did Shaun and the sheep discover they needed a shepherd?
- How did they find the shepherd?
- Why did Peter follow Jesus back to Rome?
- Why did Marcus follow Jesus?
- Whom do you follow and why?

*Father, whose Son Jesus is the Good Shepherd of your
people: Grant that when we hear His voice, we will know
Him who calls us each by name, and follow where He leads.
Amen.*

LOOKING AHEAD

Have you said or done things that you regret? See the next devotion.

17

The Most Radical Event: Our Redeemer Arrives

MOVIE THAT INSPIRES
The War of the Worlds (1953)

Have you said or done things you regret? If you have, read the good news in Isaiah 9:2–3, 6–7, which was quoted on pages 59–60.

The passage starts out focusing on a people who walked in darkness. Of course, it's referring to those who lived before the coming of the Messiah, but it also refers to all of us before we see the light.

Often, I get up at three a.m. It's hard to find the light switches, and I bump into things. But when I turn on the light, I can see the path and the obstacles. There's also spiritual darkness. Jesus, who is the Light, illuminates the way by showing us the obstacles and the path.

Jesus Christ's birth is the most radical political event in history. Seven hundred years beforehand, Isaiah predicted that the Creator God would invade our world as a child. The thought that God would come as a child is extraordinary.

The names that God gave Isaiah for Jesus are found nowhere else in the Old Testament:

Wonderful Counselor: The counselor was the king because in those days the king would make decisions. Jesus is called "Wonderful Counselor" because He makes the right decisions. He loves us so much that not only does He make the decision, but He also carries it out.

Mighty God: The Bible also says He's going to be a mighty warrior against the forces of evil.

Everlasting Father: Jesus wants to protect us and provide for us something better than we can possibly expect from the world.

Prince of Peace: Jesus wants us to have peace and well-being now.

Seven hundred years later, the event predicted by Isaiah arrived. Luke 2:1 starts the story of Jesus' birth by saying, "In those days a decree went out from Emperor Augustus that all the world should be registered" (NRSV). There has never been a story with the magnitude of the birth of Jesus Christ. The Ancient of Days, the Creator of everything in heaven and earth, came to earth as a baby. It was like an alien invasion, but by a baby who could be cuddled and hugged.

Now Jesus was born at a specific historical moment. Emperor Augustus was the first Roman emperor who overthrew the Roman Republic and established the empire by cruelty. His name means "exalted," because Augustus exalted himself and transformed the republic into the most draconian empire ever.

As Augustus was conquering, the real Emperor of the universe was born. Jesus didn't exalt Himself. He was born a baby and placed in a manger, surrounded by smelly animals in a stable. The Greek word for *manger* comes from a word that means "to eat." This is a foreshadowing of the Last Supper, when Jesus would say, "Take, eat … in remembrance of me" (see Luke 22:14–23).

In the 1953 movie adaptation of H. G. Wells' book *The War of the Worlds*, big, ugly alien Martians invade the earth and kill humans. Nothing, including nuclear weapons, can stop them. The hero and heroine and others flock to churches to pray. When the Martians die, the narrator explains, "Once they had breathed our air, germs, which no longer affect us, began to kill them. … After all that men could do had failed, the Martians were destroyed, and humanity was saved by the littlest things, which God, in His wisdom, had put upon this Earth."[4]

In contrast to science fiction books and movies, our most radical invasion was the Creator of the universe born as one of us. He gave Himself to free us from fear, pain, all the things we did wrong, and all the penalties we must pay for all the people we hurt.

Our Redeemer has paid the penalty for everything you regret and more. He is here forever to care for you, protect you, and guide you. He is here to help you, walk with you, and talk with you.

FILM TO FAITH

Watch this movie:

o   *The War of the Worlds* (1953)

Ask:

- o   How does God use the weak to bring redemption to the world in *The War of the Worlds*?
- o   How does God's redemption contrast with alien invasion and imperial rulers?
- o   Why is the birth of Jesus Christ the most radical political event ever?

Father, grant that we, who joyfully receive Jesus as our Redeemer, be used to continue to redeem our world, and with sure confidence we will behold Him when He comes to be our Judge.

LOOKING AHEAD

Do you have burdens? Do you have pains? Have you been delivered? See the next devotion.

---

4   *The War of the Worlds, IMDb,* accessed September 25, 2017, http://www.imdb.com/title/tt0046534/.

Delivered from Burdens and Pains

The King of Kings (1927)
The Young Messiah

Do you have burdens? Do you have pains? Have you been delivered?

Like a great filmmaker, God tells us exactly where His story is going a thousand years before it happened in Psalm 118 and Psalm 30. As well, Isaiah 50:4–6 was written seven hundred years before Jesus Christ came to heal and save you and me: "The LORD God has given me the tongue of a teacher, that I may know how to sustain the weary with a word. Morning by morning he wakens, wakens my ear, to listen as those who are taught. The LORD God has opened my ear, and I was not rebellious, I did not turn backward. I gave my back to those who struck me, and my cheeks to those who pulled out the beard; I did not hide my face from insult and spitting" (NRSV).

Isaiah 50 is the third of four suffering servant songs. It affirms the Messiah's faith in God. Jesus carries out God's mission in the face of ridicule and opposition, confident that God will sustain Him. Now what is He doing that causes so much trouble?

God woke Him early in the morning that day to help the weary, to heal the blind and the lame, to comfort the prisoner, and to feed the hungry. Every morning, God was giving Him new inspiration to be able to do these things, which was treating humanity with great respect whether they were Israelis or a Samaritan woman or a Gentile.

So there He was healing them, and what did He get for it? He got to be beaten like a criminal. He got his beard pulled out with contempt. He got spit on with hatred.

The intensity of the mocking of Jesus Christ is shown with great power in one of the best Jesus movies, Cecil B. DeMille's 1927 version of *The King of Kings*. Since it was a silent movie, it is said that more people around the world came to know Jesus Christ through this version than any of the other 150 movies about Jesus Christ. DeMille, the son of a pastor, wanted the movie to be extremely powerful, so he had H. B. Warner, who played Jesus, isolated from the rest of the cast and also held a prayer service every morning. Unlike the rest of the movie, which is in black and white, the scene of the resurrected Jesus appearing to the disciples is in color and is as powerful today as when it was first shown.

If you've seen many of the movies about Jesus, they include three crosses but only one has a sign on it. But at the time of the crucifixion, most of the crosses had signs on them. Why? To warn the passersby not to commit the crime written on the sign.

People were crucified all the way from Jerusalem to Caesarea on the Mediterranean coast—many miles of crucifixions. The only movie that shows that in a powerful way is *The Young Messiah*. There were so many crucifixions that you'd walk three feet and there would be another crucifixion. Most had a sign telling what the person had done, except when it came to Jesus. His sign read "The King of the Jews."

Why did Jesus endure the beatings, the mockery, and the crucifixion? To heal and save you and me. God is calling you to receive the healing, the forgiveness, and the new life. So believe, receive, and become an adopted child of God and heir of His eternal glory, knowing that Jesus was beaten, crucified, and resurrected to deliver us from our sins, burdens, and pain.

FILM TO FAITH

Watch one or both of these movies:

- *The King of Kings* (1927)
- *The Young Messiah*

Ask:

- How does *The King of Kings* show that Jesus' suffering delivered each human being from their sins, burdens, and pain?
- How does *The King of Kings* show the reality of the resurrection?
- How does *The Young Messiah* show that the young Jesus Christ was destined to die and be resurrected to deliver each human being from their sins, burdens, and pains?
- How does realizing what Jesus went through help you when you face difficult times?

Father, you gave your only begotten Son, Jesus Christ, to shed His blood to deliver me, heal me, and redeem me. Take my pain and burdens and use me to tell others about this good news.

LOOKING AHEAD

Do you need a miracle? Just what is a miracle? See the next devotion.

19

What Is a Miracle?

Unbroken
China Cry

Do you need a miracle? Just what is a miracle?

The Greek word for *miracle* comes from a root that means "sign." So a miracle is a sign pointing toward God. For most people, a miracle suggests God's supernatural intervention that surpasses the power of nature, science, or human ability.

The Bible tells us, "For nothing is impossible with God" (Luke 1:37 NLT) and "Jesus said to him, 'If you can'! All things are possible for one who believes'" (Mark 9:23 ESV). Miracles may happen quickly, over time, or perhaps years later. Before they happen, miracles appear to be impossible, such as the healing of an incurable disease. And afterward, many people try to explain them away or attribute them to unique and unexpected natural events.

In the biopic *Unbroken*, Louis Zamperini (Jack O'Connell) and two other crew members survive the crash of their rickety old plane in World War II, only to be stranded at sea on a raft for forty-seven days, many of the later days without food or water. In a crucial moment when a violent storm rages, Louie cries out to God and promises to serve Him for the rest of his life if he survives. Louie survives but is found by the Japanese, and the two remaining men are thrown into a prisoner of war camp where they are tortured and abused.

Louie's prayer is answered miraculously, but the miracle at sea becomes the miracle in the Japanese concentration camp, and then the miracle back in the United States when he finally accepts Jesus Christ as his Savior and becomes one of the twentieth century's great evangelists, fulfilling his promise to God. The movie only hints at the entire miracle, but it still affirms the sign of God's providential intervention.

The one triune God impacts our lives miraculously far more often than we realize. However, if we believe that miracles still occur and thank God for all the little miracles in our lives, we often experience more of His divine, sovereign grace.

In another biopic, *China Cry*, Sung Neng Yee (Julia Nickson), who later becomes Nora Lam, is a young Chinese communist who gets caught up in the horrors of Mao's Cultural Revolution program to torture people to reeducate them. When all seems lost, she prays to Jesus: "I talked to you when I was a child. Do you remember my name?" Miracles begin to occur, starting with lightning striking the firing squad about to shoot her so she escapes death. The rest of the story involves God's intervention in miraculous ways, leading to Nora's escape from communist China.

God is still willing and able to do miracles. They are recorded in his Word and in the lives of the Christians throughout history. He is all-powerful. He is love, and He loves us. His desire to respond to all of us who call on the name of Jesus Christ hasn't changed (see Mark 1:40–43).

Our need for miracles hasn't changed either, although we seem to have better medicine, more scientific advances, and better living conditions. People still battle incurable diseases, unemployment, life-threatening disasters, accidents, poverty, painful relationships, demons, mental disorders, disobedient children, broken marriages, death, and a desperate need for Jesus Christ (see Matthew 9:35–38; 15:32–38).

God knows that people still need to see what Jesus Christ can do. He's glorified by revealing His love in and through miracles. Seeing what Christ can do helps people put their faith in Him and receive life's greatest of miracles—salvation, being born again with eternal life through the forgiveness of sin (Matthew 15:29–31).

FILM TO FAITH

Watch one or both of these movies:

- *Unbroken*
- *China Cry*

Ask:

- How do Louis Zamperini and Nora Lam experience signs pointing toward God?
- How did God intervene in *Unbroken* and *China Cry* in ways that surpass the power of nature, science, or human ability?
- Why did Louis Zamperini need God to intervene?
- Why did Nora Lam need God to intervene?
- What do *Unbroken* and *China Cry* teach you about miracles and about God?

Father, I know that your ways are not my ways and that I cannot manipulate you to do my will, but I need a sign of your presence. Please show up in my life and help me in Jesus Christ's name.

LOOKING AHEAD

Do you want your children to love one another, rather than lust after people and things? See the next devotion.

20

Love vs. Lust
(and Tolerance)

MOVIES THAT INSPIRE

Frozen
Runaway Bride

Do you want your children to love one another, rather than lust after people and things?

Tolerating self-destructive or socially destructive behavior in our children is not a sign of love, but neglect. If a child has a propensity to beat themselves or other children, parents are required by love to intervene to help the child get over such intolerable behavior.

God calls us all to love our neighbor as ourselves: "I am not writing a new commandment for you; rather, it is an old one you have had from the very beginning. This old commandment—to love one another" (1 John 2:7 NLT).

That divine call entails helping ourselves and our neighbors get over destructive behavior, such as violence against the innocent, alcoholic stupors, and perverting our children's innocent hearts and minds, by frankly intervening and correcting such behavior in a manner that brings about significant change or repentance (see Leviticus 19:17–18).

The movie *Frozen*, which extols Christian love, is a profound visual story about four types of love (note that there are six ancient Greek words for love). The opening music, "Vuelie," fore-shadows this as a combination of an ancient Norwegian Sami yoik and the Danish Christian hymn "Dejlig er jorden" ("Fairest Lord Jesus").

Cursed by the magical ability to freeze everything, Princess Elsa withdraws into self-love (*philautia*), which almost destroys the town. The dashing Prince Hans of the Southern Isles shows the destructive force of lustful romantic love (*eros*). Olaf, the cheerful snowman, shows the weakness of the love demonstrated in friendship (*philia*). However, it is only Anna's selfless, sacrificial, loving intervention (*agape*) that can thaw a frozen heart.

The foundation of Christianity (ontology) is one of love. It says we live in a real world, created by the real God, where there are real problems, real pain, and real suffering, and where we need a real Savior, Jesus Christ, who loves us so much that He frees us from the bondage of lusts, sin, anxieties, burdens, and other negative forces.

In the movie *Runaway Bride*, Maggie Carpenter (Julia Roberts) keeps getting engaged and proceeding all the way to the altar only to run away at the last minute. Her problem is that she keeps trying to please each fiancé, ignoring the real essence of Christian marriage, which is to make a commitment in the sight of God and man for the right reasons, not just romantic reasons.

A Christian worldview is love in action, and a pagan worldview is lust in action. Love gives; lust takes. Love empowers; lust destroys. Love saves; lust enslaves. Love marks the freedom of the abundant life (as promised by Jesus Christ) built on the fruit of the Holy Spirit.

True love affirms life. True love gives. True love shares. True love does not delight in evil or sinful behavior, including extramarital lust. Lust, on the other hand, consumes. It takes without permission. Lust is never satisfied.

We have moved from a society of love to a society of lust, where we tolerate evil in the name of self-gratification, or in the name of trying not to "offend" another person. We need to exercise love by refusing to tolerate the evils destroying our culture and jeopardizing the future of our children and grandchildren.

What can we possibly give our children and grandchildren that is more valuable than that—a culture that honors Jesus Christ and His gospel of true love? Nothing!

FILM TO FAITH

Watch one or both of these movies:

- *Frozen*
- *Runaway Bride*

Ask:

- How does *Frozen* commend selfless Christian love?
- How does Anna refuse to tolerate Elsa's self-love?
- How does Ike show real love to Maggie in *Runaway Bride*?
- How does Maggie learn to love others as herself?
- What types of love are you showing in your life?

Father, help me and my family to know your love, as manifested in the free gift of new life offered by Jesus Christ. Help us not to espouse "I don't care what you do" tolerance instead of love, and fill us with your fruit of the Holy Spirit: love, joy, peace, patience, kindness, goodness, faith, gentleness, and self-control.

LOOKING AHEAD

Do you have great plans that seem to be waiting for God's approval? See the next devotion.

Our Attitudes vs.
Our Accomplishments

MOVIES THAT INSPIRE
Stanley and Livingstone
The Queen

Do you have great plans that seem to be waiting for God's approval? Do you sense that you're being transformed by the fruit of the Spirit?

God sends us into the world as victors to make a tremendous difference. He tells us this in Romans 8:37: "No, in all these things we are more than conquerors through him who loved us" (NRSV).

Previously, we talked about how God's will for us is that He wants us to be happy, to talk to Him, and to be grateful. He also wants us to exhibit the fruit of the Spirit, as Paul specifies in Galatians 5:22–23: "By contrast, the fruit of the Spirit is love, joy, peace, patience, kindness, generosity, faithfulness, gentleness, and self-control. There is no law against such things" (NRSV).

So God is more concerned with our attitudes than our accomplishments. Although He wants us to be more than conquerors, He's concerned about our attitude. He wants us to have the humility to know that none of this came from our own doing, but from His grace.

Dr. David Livingstone was an achiever. At a young age, he taught himself to read as he worked in dangerous conditions at a factory. Then he put himself through medical school. In 1840, he was inspired to go into the mission field of Africa to get rid of the slave trade and bring people to Christ.

However, it didn't work out that way. For years, Dr. Livingstone endured one disaster after another. The Royal Geographic Society gave up on him after he brought a group of noblemen into Africa, took them up the Zambezi River, and some of them got killed. His children died. His wife became an alcoholic and died. He had nothing to show for all his mission work.

Then, as the 1939 movie *Stanley and Livingstone* depicts, Stanley (Spencer Tracy), a real rascal of a reporter, set out to find Livingstone (Cedric Hardwicke). Nobody had heard from him in three years, and many people thought he was dead. Stanley's whole purpose was to show that Livingstone was a charlatan and a fraud. Instead, Stanley found a gentle, white-haired man who had only a few months to live. Stanley was so impressed with Livingstone's loving heart that, although no one else had come to Christ through his ministry, Stanley did.

Stanley went on to write the book *Through the Dark Continent*, which helped stop the slave trade. Revival broke out in the part of Africa where Livingstone was, and it continues to this very day. Now God wanted Livingston to be more than a conqueror, but it wasn't until his attitude got in line with godly virtues that he was able to achieve what God had appointed for him.

The same providential character arc can be seen in the movie *The Queen*. When Princess Diana (Laurence Burg) is killed in a car accident in Paris, Queen Elizabeth II (Helen Mirren) exhibits a stiff upper lip to address the suffering of the nation. The Queen comes to realize her attitude must exhibit the fruit of the Holy Spirit, since the nation has changed during her reign. When she does change her attitude, she wins the hearts and minds of the people.

Hallmark uses the slogan "When You Care Enough to Send

the Very Best."[5] The most important word in this phrase is *enough*. Do you care *enough* to change your attitude? Do you care *enough* to walk in the attitudes of humility and grace in conversation with your Creator?

God is empowering you and waiting for you to do just that.

FILM TO FAITH

Watch one or both of these movies:

- *Stanley and Livingstone*
- *The Queen*

Ask:

- How did God use Dr. Livingstone to transform Stanley?
- What did Stanley do after meeting Dr. Livingstone?
- How did Queen Elizabeth II realize she needed to change her attitude?
- How did the people of the United Kingdom change when Queen Elizabeth II changed?
- How has your attitude been changed by the fruit of the Spirit?

Father, you put the desire on my heart to do mighty things for your kingdom. Please transform me to be worthy of being the instrument of your good news by building the fruit of the Spirit into my character.

LOOKING AHEAD

How can you make the good news of the Bible come alive for your family and friends? Are there fantasy movies that can be watched from a biblical perspective? See the next devotion.

---

5   "Brand Legacy," *Hallmark*, accessed September 26, 2017, https://corporate .hallmark.com/OurBrand/Brand-Legacy.

22

Fantasy Movies and the Bible

MOVIES THAT INSPIRE

The Lord of the Rings series
The Chronicles of Narnia series

How can you make the good news of the Bible come alive for your family and friends? Are there fantasy movies that can be watched from a biblical perspective?

The Bible is a wonderful library of histories, prophecies, biographies, parables, reflections, instructions, and wisdom, both transcendent and immanent. Its various parts have shaped almost every aspect of culture and civilization, including movies. In fact, a good movie story is a journey toward God. It reminds us of the Master Storyteller.

Biblical (and even explicitly Christian) themes abound even in fantasy movies, as Peter Jackson's *The Lord of the Rings* movies attest. *The Lord of the Rings* movies especially are rife with allegorical references to heaven, redemption, the kingdom of heaven on earth, refutation of paganism and evil, and commendation of honor, duty, decency, and loyalty, all of which J. R. R. Tolkien intentionally incorporated into his original book, which his publisher released as a trilogy. As conversations with his friend C. S. Lewis confirm, Tolkien sought to exalt the Christian life and the call to greatness through faith.

Contemporary fantasy movies such as *The Chronicles of Narnia* series, based on C. S. Lewis' famous children's books, clearly reveal biblical truths and even the essence of the gospel itself, and so influence the reception of the Bible.

Although Lewis didn't intend to give a one-to-one correlation to the gospel of Jesus Christ, *The Lion, the Witch and the Wardrobe* is a compelling allegory that leads the reader to a deeper understanding of the good news of the gospel. Through it, Lewis brings to life a critical verse in Scripture: "For God so loved the world that He gave His only begotten Son, that whoever believes in Him should not perish but have everlasting life" (John 3:16 NKJV).

In the story, the lion Aslan, son of the Emperor-beyond-the-Sea, gives his life to pay the death penalty for a human boy, Edmund, who became a traitor to his family and to all that was good in Narnia. Edmund is to be put to death for betraying his family by joining the company of the evil White Witch in order to gorge himself on Turkish Delight. Aslan rescues Edmund by dying in Edmund's place; Edmund is set free while Aslan is resurrected. Transformed by the love that Aslan showed him, Edmund joins the company of Aslan for the good of Narnia.

C. S. Lewis' book was inspired by a true story. Two thousand years ago, Jesus sacrificed His life to pay the penalty of humanity's betrayal of God. He is the Son of the true God. Like Edmund, we all have betrayed God by rebelling against Him and deserve a death penalty for it. "All have sinned and fall short of the glory of God" (Romans 3:23). But Jesus, through His sacrifice, rescued us by dying in our place. If we trust in Him, we are set free, transformed by His love to join God's company for the good of our world.

However, sin isn't only a problem for characters in novels and people in the newspapers; it's a problem for all of us. Stop and think over your day. Whose desires were the most important in the decisions you made? If the answer is not God's desires, you have a problem with sin. The good news is that God has made a way for you to be set free from the bondage to sin and death.

The Bible speaks of how much God loves us and wants us to be transformed: "God showed his great love for us by sending Christ to die for us while we were still sinners" (Romans 5:8 NLT). He loves each of us in spite of our betrayal of Him as sinners. In fact, God's love is powerful enough to redeem us from our death penalty.

Since the earliest days of moviemaking, many movies have explicitly and implicitly intended to help open the audience to the Bible. These movies can bring alive the good news of the Bible for your family and friends, if they are watched with a biblical perspective.

FILM TO FAITH

Watch one or both of these movie series:

- *The Lord of the Rings* series
- *The Chronicles of Narnia* series

Ask:

- How do *The Lord of the Rings* movies reference heaven, redemption, the kingdom of heaven on earth, refutation of paganism and evil, and commendation of honor, duty, decency, and loyalty?
- How do *The Lord of the Rings* movies exalt the Christian life and the call to greatness through faith?
- How do *The Chronicles of Narnia* movies reveal biblical truths?
- How do *The Chronicles of Narnia* movies reveal the essence of the gospel itself?

- How can *The Chronicles of Narnia* series and *The Lord of the Rings* series be used to influence the reception of the Bible?

Father, please help my family and friends to open themselves to the Bible through movies like The Chronicles of Narnia *series and* The Lord of the Rings *series, and please help them to see the good news of the Bible in these wonderful movies.*

LOOKING AHEAD

Has a movie helped you to know more about Jesus Christ? Do you have a favorite movie about Him that has inspired you to a better life? See the next devotion.

23

Jesus
in the Movies

MOVIES THAT INSPIRE

The Jesus Film

The Gospel According to St. Matthew (1964)

Has a movie helped you to know more about Jesus Christ? Do you have a favorite movie about Him that has inspired you to a better life?

As the Master Storyteller, Jesus knew the power stories have to teach, influence, and inspire. He often spoke in parables, which are short fictitious stories illustrating a moral principle or a religious doctrine.

Movies are like parables in that they too can illustrate moral principles and religious doctrines, including beliefs about God and Jesus Christ that enhance and influence the reception of the Bible. Since Jesus told parables that taught principles and doctrines that are good, true, and beautiful, these movies should follow suit. They shouldn't contradict what the Bible teaches, including its moral principles.

According to *Frodo & Harry: Understanding Visual Media and Its Impact on Our Lives* by Ted Baehr and Tom Snyder, a myth is "any real or fictional story, recurring theme, or character type that appeals to the consciousness of a people by embodying major cultural ideals and/or by giving expression to deep, commonly felt, and/or transcendent emotions and/or rational or irrational ideas."[6] The story of the hero is one such myth, and it can occur in either fiction or nonfiction.

Of course, the greatest hero story is that of Jesus Christ, who died for our sins but rose from the dead by an act of God, and who offers us a personal relationship with God. This relationship, empowered by communion and fellowship with the Holy Spirit, leads us into all truth, and eventually will lead us into eternal life with the one true God—the Father, Son, and Holy Spirit.

The earliest representations of Jesus on film were straightforward, primitive movies of live Passion plays about the crucifixion. These plays were some of the longest movies made during their time, and they were so successful that they eventually convinced the Nickelodeon operators that there was an audience not just for shorts, but also for longer, feature-length movies. In part, the modern movie was birthed out of the overwhelming success of the Passion plays.

In 1897, two American theatrical producers, Marc Klaw and Abraham Erlanger, filmed a Passion play in Horitz, Bohemia. A year later, R. G. Holloman and A. G. Eaves filmed a Passion play on the roof of the Grand Central Palace in New York. Also in that year, the Oberammergau Passion Play was filmed by a Mr. Hurd, an American representative of the first major French filmmakers, the Lumière brothers, and a French Passion play was filmed for the Eden Musée.

When reflecting on how Hollywood movies and television programs have presented Jesus Christ, it's important to keep in mind that Matthew, Mark, Luke, and John wrote gospels, not scripts. Their narratives about Jesus inspire and teach through

---

6   Ted Baehr and Tom Snyder, *Frodo & Harry: Understanding Visual Media and Its Impact on Our Lives* (Grand Rapids: Crossway Books, 2003), 120. See also *Myth Conceptions*, by Tom Snyder (Grand Rapids: Baker Books, 1995).

images created by words. The filmmakers who have tackled this sensitive subject have attempted to interpret and portray Jesus through nonverbal images. Regrettably, more often than not, the most important aspect of Jesus Christ's life, His resurrection, has been ignored, though a few movies have presented the resurrection accurately and with reverence.

Each filmmaker has visualized Jesus differently. Some have stuck close to the story of a particular gospel, while others have held to the theme of the gospel. Some have used the figure of Jesus to tell their own personal stories, while others have used gospel stories as a pretext for presenting popular ideologies. Unfortunately, some filmmakers have made movies about Jesus because they wanted to make money, and some have done so because they wanted to mock or defame Him. Others have a passion to tell the real story of Christ's life.

Jesus can be portrayed not only as an indigenous Jew, but also in the abstract. Furthermore, there are Christ figures as well as Jesus figures. A Jesus figure is any representation of Jesus Himself, which can be realistic or stylized. A Christ figure, however, is a character who portrays or symbolizes an important aspect of Christ's nature or His life and ministry. When the representation of a Jesus figure is realistic, such as in *The Jesus Film*, then it is Jesus as He actually was thought to be. To do so means looking at Jesus from the perspective of His time, not ours.

Most film representations of Jesus figures, however, tend to rely on well-known visual portraits of Him from the European Renaissance. These portraits tend to soften Jesus (though Pasolini's *The Gospel According to St. Matthew* [1964] leans heavily on Renaissance church paintings and yet presents a real Jesus). They present Him in non-historical settings, just as Italian Medieval and Renaissance art presented Him in Italian settings.

Each of the more than 150 movies about Jesus Christ has its own appeal and insights, although a few are unorthodox and contrary to sound biblical doctrine and all, like sermons, have their own vision of Jesus Christ. Many of these movies can help you know more about Him and inspire you to a better life.

FILM TO FAITH

Watch one or both of these movies:

- *The Jesus Film*
- *The Gospel According to St. Matthew* (1964)

Ask:

- How was Jesus Christ portrayed in each movie?
- How did each movie help you to understand Jesus Christ better?
- How did each movie inspire you?

Father, I want to know Jesus better, love Him more, and be inspired by Him. Please help me to see the good and reject the bad in movies about Jesus Christ, by the power of your Holy Spirit.

LOOKING AHEAD

Have you watched a movie and thought that the hero's qualities remind you of Jesus Christ? See the next devotion.

Christ
in the Movies

MOVIES THAT INSPIRE

Strange Cargo
Jesus Christ Superstar

Have you watched a movie and thought that the hero's qualities remind you of Jesus Christ? Have you been touched by the stories of Christ figures?

In contrast to Jesus figures, Christ figures are often people who are either redeemers or saviors. The redeemer figure represents Jesus taking on human burdens and sinfulness in suffering and even death. For example, John Coffey (Michael Clarke Duncan) in *The Green Mile* is both a "holy fool" and a Christ figure who bears the sins of others to his own death. The savior figure portrays Jesus' saving mission, sometimes even to triumph in a symbolic or actual resurrection.

Other Christ figures are:

- A martyr figure whose suffering and death witnesses to values and convictions
- A Job-like figure who is innocent but suffers and is persecuted
- A popular savior such as a legendary knight or a contemporary pop hero

- A clown figure who highlights the fact that God's folly is wiser than human wisdom
- A reconciler figure who brings enemies together

Movies may also portray Jesus as a teacher, wonder-worker, all-powerful Creator, monk, human, or risen Lord. This is acceptable if the Christology is orthodox (correct in doctrine). An orthodox Christology requires at least:

- A real ontology, which means that reality is real, not just a great thought or something else
- A real epistemology, which means that a person can really know that reality is real
- A real soteriology, which means that Jesus really saved us
- A real resurrection
- A real divinity, which means that Jesus is God
- A real incarnational theology, which means that Jesus was fully God and fully man
- A real history, which means that Jesus' death and resurrection are actual events in history
- A real morality, which means that Jesus died once for the sins of all
- A real victory, which means Jesus' death was not a defeat but a triumph

Using an obvious Christ figure, the 1940 movie *Strange Cargo* is an unusual and well-acted fantasy redemption drama with strong performances. The plot follows a group of convicts from their prison break to their deaths, or final "escapes." The Christ figure serves as the collective conscience with whom each has to deal with or deny.

The story portrays prisoners from Devil's Island who come back from a day of work and find an extra man, Cambreau (Ian

Hunter), in their midst. He seems to have supernatural knowledge of the other convicts' lives and seeks to develop their better natures. As a cynical unbeliever, André Verne (Clark Gable), hurls the stranger into the sea during a quarrel. The stranger clutches a wooden plank, assuming a crucifixion-like posture. Verne realizes who the stranger is and is converted to belief in God, and the stranger disappears.

In 1973, two fanciful musicals presented the gospel of Jesus Christ. *Jesus Christ Superstar*, adapted from the musical by Tim Rice and Andrew Lloyd Webber, presents a Jesus figure, using the musical idioms of the 1960s. Director Norman Jewison's movie adaptation was more reverent and even hinted at the resurrection.

This modern retelling of the gospel story sets Christianity on edge by partially turning the villains of the story into the heroes. Used by God to accomplish His purpose, Judas is presented as noble and knowledgeable, though angry, and Pontius Pilate is a troubled man who has premonitions of the truth about Jesus and his own role in His death.

Godspell is another 1960s rock opera retelling of the story of Jesus in a New York setting. It uses a Jesus clown figure to summarize the life and death of Christ according to the Gospel of Matthew. Regrettably, the movie reflects the brief ascendance of the humanization of Jesus promoted by the German school of higher criticism and avoids the divinity of Christ and His resurrection.

Nearly every year, movies are released embodying Christian references and allusions, such as *Man of Steel*, *The Hunger Games: Catching Fire*, and *The Croods*. For example, Superman goes to church to confess in *Man of Steel*. Love and self-sacrifice become the spiritual weapons wielded against socialist tyranny in *The Hunger Games: Catching Fire*. And the Neolithic family in *The Croods* take a leap of faith to "follow the Light."

So movies can highlight and feature an aspect of what makes Jesus of Nazareth the Christ. We can learn from and be inspired by these references and allusions. One viewer of CBS-TV's 1980 version of *The Lion, the Witch and the Wardrobe* wrote that he had been told about the sacrificial death of Jesus Christ all his life, but he never understood it until he watched Aslan die on the Stone Table for Edmund.

By watching movies with Christ figures, you can be inspired and can help others meet and know the risen Savior.

FILM TO FAITH

Watch one or both of these movies:

- *Strange Cargo*
- *Jesus Christ Superstar*

Ask:

- How is Cambreau in *Strange Cargo* a Christ figure?
- What does *Strange Cargo* teach you about Christ?
- How does *Jesus Christ Superstar* reflect the gospel?
- How does *Jesus Christ Superstar* veer off the gospel story?
- What does *Jesus Christ Superstar* teach you about Christ?

Father, help me to discern the truth of Jesus Christ in allegorical and other movies that present Christ figures, and to not be led astray by false doctrine. Help people see more of the nature of Christ in me.

LOOKING AHEAD

Are you ever concerned about what's in your future? Would you like to know how to make your future better? See the next devotion.

25

Be the Light of the World

By David Outten[7]

MOVIES THAT INSPIRE
Back to the Future II
Doctor Zhivago

Are you ever concerned about what's in your future? Would you like to know how to make your future better? Would you like to know how to make the world better?

Obviously, not all movies inspire just by modeling sweetness and light. It's important to be able to learn inspiring lessons from movies that show the negative impact of evil. While the *Back to the Future* trilogy has some content Movieguide® would warn against, these movies were very popular because, with great spunk, Doc and Marty explored the impact of decisions and actions on the future you experience.

In *Back to the Future II*, Doc and Marty return to 1985 from 2015. They find a hellish Hill Valley with Biff's Pleasure Palace at its center. It's an ugly segment, with the community awash in violence, pollution, and anger. Doc explains to Marty that somewhere in the past, the time continuum must have veered into a horrible alternate reality.

The problem was that in 2015, Biff took the time machine and

---

7   Editor's note: David Outten is an artist and writer and longtime friend of Dr. Ted Baehr. Like Ted, he is passionate about leaving a better world for his children and grandchildren.

traveled back to 1955. He gave the younger Biff an almanac with sports scores in it, and this enabled the 1955 Biff to become the wealthy and powerful Biff of 1985. What makes this such a great lesson is that you see in a profound way the negative impact of character flaws like greed, lust, and pride. They don't just make Biff a miserable person; they impact culture.

The classic David Lean movie *Doctor Zhivago* contains adultery and other material Movieguide® does not condone, but it profoundly shows the negative impact of bad beliefs on culture. It opens with a young Zhivago as a member of Moscow high society before the communist revolution. Later we see the impact of the revolution on his life. It's horrible—even worse than Biff's 1985 Hill Valley—but it's historically accurate. Millions of people suffered.

Our future is not determined just by what we do. We live in a culture shaped by others.

Jesus Christ came not only to invite people to experience eternal life in heaven, but also to radically transform culture. The reason we don't live in Biff's Hill Valley or a communist gulag is because our culture has been profoundly shaped by people with good values.

Jesus told his followers, "You are the light of the world" (Matthew 5:14 NRSV). We're called to be a good influence, which includes working diligently to influence the entertainment industry to promote what's good.

Jesus also said, "You are the salt of the earth. But if the salt loses its saltiness, how can it be made salty again? It is no longer good for anything, except to be thrown out and trampled underfoot" (Matthew 5:13). What He's saying is that if good people don't do their part to influence culture for the good, they'll wind up living in a culture driven by evil. In such a culture, good people get trampled.

Being the light of the world begins with being a light in your own family and community. You become a light when you model the fruit of the Spirit (love, joy, peace, forbearance, kindness, goodness, faithfulness, gentleness, and self-control).

Imagine what a wonderful place Hill Valley would be if people living there were filled with the fruit of the Spirit. And imagine what Doctor Zhivago's life could have been like if he hadn't failed in the area of faithfulness. His adultery cost him his wife and children. People's actions impact others.

You are the light of the world when you impact others for good. What's wonderful is that the greater the good influence you have on others, the more joy you experience. Consider Acts 20:35: "In everything I did, I showed you that by this kind of hard work we must help the weak, remembering the words the Lord Jesus Himself said: 'It is more blessed to give than to receive.'" Being a light in the world actually brings joy.

You will not be fondly remembered in life for the things you got for yourself. You will be remembered for what you did for others. Ask yourself, *How can I be a light today*?

FILM TO FAITH

Watch one or both of these movies:

- *Back to the Future II*
- *Doctor Zhivago*

Ask:

- What would make Hill Valley an ideal place to live?
- What impact did Communism have on Russia?
- What impact has Christianity had on America?
- What makes your community better or worse?

- What can you do to make your community better?
- What impact will you have on culture?

Father, I thank you that I don't live in Biff's Hill Valley or in Communist North Korea. Thank you for all those who use your light to shape America. Help me to be a light other countries and a good influence on society.

LOOKING AHEAD

Do you consider humility a key to success? See the next devotion.

26

The Rewards of Humility

By David Outten

MOVIES THAT INSPIRE

Cars

Pride & Prejudice (2005)

Do you consider humility a key to success?

In the Pixar movie *Cars*, humility was the last thing Lightning McQueen considered a key to success, but the whole point of the movie was to teach him that it is. He could win races with his speed, but he didn't win friends. He was arrogant and prideful when he wound up in the small town of Radiator Springs, and he hated being stuck in a backwoods town full of nobodies. By the end of the movie, however, McQueen chooses kindness over victory and wins many more friends than he ever could have by winning the race.

1 Peter 5:5 says, "God opposes the proud but shows favor to the humble." To be humble doesn't mean that you think you're worthless or inferior. It means that even with amazing abilities, you don't act as if you're more valuable than others. God loves the rich and the poor, the astrophysicist and farmer, the athlete and the nerd. He'd have us love others regardless of what they do or what their gifts are. He has the abilities of God, but He loves even those who have made a horrible mess of their life.

In the 2005 version of *Pride and Prejudice*, we get a more adult view of the dangers of pride. In this case, a relatively poor girl named Elizabeth Bennet (Keira Knightley) is too proud to show interest in a wealthy man named Mr. Darcy (Matthew Macfadyen) because she mistakenly considers him unkind. In a delightful twist, she discovers that his behavior was actually both kind and noble. She learns a great lesson and gets a wonderful husband.

Humility is not despair or feeling worthless. It's actually feeling powerful without being puffed up with pride. When you know your talents and abilities come from God's grace, you can walk in them and pass the glory on to Him.

There are two reasons you should consider humility a key to success: 1) God blesses the humble; and 2) People love to work with those who have great ability but don't act as if they're better than others. These two benefits often lead to wealth and honor. Consider Proverbs 22:4: "The reward for humility and fear of the LORD is riches and honor and life" (ESV).

At the end of *Cars*, Lightning McQueen has a devoted pit crew because he's learned to value each of them. No one wishes to be treated as an inferior to be commanded and demanded. Everyone wants to be appreciated. The humble person appreciates others.

The team that wins a World Series or Super Bowl is seldom one where the players consider themselves more important than their teammates. Life is a team sport, and success is rarely accomplished alone. When people respect those who work with them and build each other up, much more is accomplished.

Simply put, humility pleases God and brings personal satisfaction. The prideful person lives in constant pursuit of the next award or payday. The humble person lives in pursuit of an opportunity to bless others. The prideful person will wind up losing; no one wins all the time. The humble person will never run out of people to bless; their happiness is not dependent on trophies, though they may well win some.

Don't forget that God has spiritual laws similar to physical laws. The law of gravity says that if you jump in the air, you'll soon come back down. The law of humility is spelled out in Matthew 23:12: "Whoever exalts himself will be humbled, and whoever humbles himself will be exalted" (ESV).

Both Lightning McQueen in *Cars* and Elizabeth in *Pride & Prejudice* learn and enjoy the benefits of humility, but both learn their lessons the hard way. It's far better to learn it from a good movie than from personal mistakes. Proverbs 16:18 gives a warning that remains true even after three thousand years: "Pride goes before destruction, a haughty spirit before a fall" (NKJV).

FILM TO FAITH

Watch one or both of these movies:

- *Cars*
- *Pride & Prejudice* (2005)

Ask:

- Why would you prefer to be Lightning McQueen's friend at the end of the movie rather than the beginning?
- How can poor people be too proud?
- How will humility help you be a better friend?
- What benefits do you expect from being humble?

Father, you deserve all glory. Help me to model humility. Help me to respect everyone as a person you love. Help me to be a great coworker who lifts others up. Thank you for revealing to me your keys to happiness.

LOOKING AHEAD

Do you wish you were more beautiful? See the next devotion.

God's Beauty Secret Revealed

By David Outten

MOVIES THAT INSPIRE
Gone With the Wind
Cinderella (2015)

If you're female, do you wish you were more beautiful? God—and two movies—can show you what true beauty is.

In *Gone with the Wind*, Scarlett O'Hara (Vivien Leigh), is stunningly beautiful. She plays with men's hearts with her flirting, but she isn't happy. She can't get over the fact that Ashley (Leslie Howard) chose Melanie (Olivia de Havilland) over herself. Some may feel that Melanie's physical appearance isn't as attractive as Scarlett's, but she is beautiful in a much more powerful way: she is kind, generous, and forgiving. She has beautiful character.

In the 2015 live-drama version of *Cinderella*, Ella is pretty, but what really makes her attractive is her humility, patience, courage, and kindness. She even ends the story with an act of forgiveness. What the prince found most attractive about her was her character. She stood out from all the other girls who were anxious to marry him for his wealth and fame.

Why does a girl or a woman wish to be beautiful? To attract a boy? For popularity? Actually, such motives are unattractive and dangerous.

To purposefully attract boys with your appearance is likely to bring a collection of boys who will make lousy husbands. A relationship with just one woman will never satisfy them.

Age becomes a lifelong enemy if self-worth is rooted in looking attractive to others. Consider Melanie in *Gone with the Wind*. Had she lived to be ninety-five, she would have been seen by others as more and more beautiful with age. She would have been much happier than Scarlett, who was at risk of becoming an old, unpleasant woman.

The greatest beauty secret of all is to measure beauty the way God does: "Your beauty should not come from outward adornment, such as elaborate hairstyles and the wearing of gold jewelry or fine clothes. Rather, it should be that of your inner self, the unfading beauty of a gentle and quiet spirit, which is of great worth in God's sight" (1 Peter 3:3–4).

It's also of great worth in a marriage and a family. The young man who longs for a beautiful wife needs the eyes of God if he wants a happy marriage: "The LORD does not look at the things people look at. People look at the outward appearance, but the LORD looks at the heart" (1 Samuel 16:7). When you look at the heart, you see something that can change. A woman does not get to choose the physical traits she inherits from her parents, but every girl is born with a heart that can be made beautiful. God is in the makeover business. He specializes in heart-lifts.

If you wish to be more beautiful tomorrow, look for ways to be a blessing to others. Find ways to compliment people for what good you see in them. Find little ways to be of assistance, even it's just returning a shopping cart to the store. Be thoughtful of others.

Behavior does more to make you beautiful than makeup ever will. The classically beautiful movie star Audrey Hepburn once said, "Make-up can only make you look pretty on the outside, but it doesn't help if you're ugly on the inside."[8]

What is uglier—a pimple or an insult? If you're known for gossiping and spewing insults, you can be pimple-free and people will still consider you ugly. Stunning beauty is found as people of any age are kind, compassionate, selfless, and joyful.

When someone sees you coming, they *recognize* you from your physical appearance, but their *opinion* of you relates more to your character. If they don't know you, then your countenance and the way you dress will give them clues to your character. How are you presenting your character to others?

God's beauty secrets are not just for women. God desires men with beautiful hearts too. Six-pack abs are just a source of trouble if the heart is filled with pride and rage. Truly beautiful women tend to look for a truly beautiful husband.

FILM TO FAITH

Watch one or both of these movies:

- *Gone With the Wind*
- *Cinderella* (2015)

8   Emma Ciufo, "The Quotable Aesthete: Audrey Hepburn," *Harper's Bazaar*, April 29, 2013, accessed September 26, 2017, http://www.harpersbazaar.com.au/celebrity /the-quotable-aesthete-audrey-hepburn-12144.

Ask:

- How and why would Melanie make a better wife than Scarlett?
- How and why was Melanie happier than Scarlett?
- What qualities most impressed the prince about Cinderella?
- How and why did Cinderella forgive her stepmother?
- What impact does forgiveness have on beauty?
- What can you do to be beautiful inside?

Father, thank you for making me beautiful from the inside out. I pray that you would help my attitude to be beautiful in your eyes. May I glow with the love you give me to share with others.

LOOKING AHEAD

Why is the resurrection of Jesus so important? See the next devotion.

28

Why the Resurrection Is Important

MOVIES THAT INSPIRE
The King of Kings (1927)
Jesus

Why is the resurrection of Jesus so important?

Although the gospel starts with Genesis and goes through Revelation, the pivotal point is the crucifixion, death, and resurrection of Jesus Christ. It is through His death that the penalty for each and every man and woman's transgressions was paid, and it is through His resurrection that He signed, sealed, and delivered the victory over sin and death once and for all.

Prior to Jesus' resurrection, the disciples were ready to run away and abandon Him. After His resurrection, they (and many others throughout the centuries) were willing to sacrifice everything for Him. For that reason, how filmmakers treat the resurrection of Jesus is extremely important.

As Paul notes:

But if it is preached that Christ has been raised from the dead, how can some of you say that there is no resurrection of the dead? If there is no resurrection of the dead, then not even Christ has been raised. And if Christ has not been raised, our preaching is useless and so is your faith. More than that, we are then found to be false witnesses about

God, for we have testified about God that he raised Christ from the dead. But he did not raise him if in fact the dead are not raised. For if the dead are not raised, then Christ has not been raised either. And, if Christ has not been raised, your faith is futile; you are still in your sins. Then those also who have fallen asleep in Christ are lost. If only for this life we have hope in Christ, we are to be pitied more than all men. But Christ has indeed been raised from the dead, the firstfruits of those who have fallen asleep. For since death came through a man, the resurrection of the dead comes also through a man. For as in Adam all die, so in Christ all will be made alive. But each in his own turn: Christ, the firstfruits; then, when he comes, those who belong to him. (1 Corinthians 15:12–23).

Like Jews, Christians believe that we live in a real world (not an imaginary world as Hindus and many others believe), that we have a real God, and that we face real suffering. Christians also believe that Jesus truly died and was resurrected. The various movies about Jesus reflect different attitudes about who Jesus was mainly by how they portray His resurrection.

One of the most renowned early movies to feature part of the life of Jesus Christ was D. W. Griffith's movie *Intolerance* (1916), which studiously avoided the resurrection. In contrast, DeMille's 1927 classic, *The King of Kings*, shows the resurrection and Thomas putting his fingers into Jesus' hands and side, saying, "My Lord—and my God!"

After DeMille's classic, many of the movies about Jesus had severe theological problems, such as *The Greatest Story Ever Told*, *Jesus Christ Superstar*, and *Godspell*. (Fortunately, several more faithful attempts at movies about Jesus followed, such as the movie *Jesus*.)

The Greatest Story Ever Told, for instance, appears to have a gnostic resurrection where an ethereal Jesus—not the physically real Jesus—appears to the disciples. Also, the language used is not the orthodox biblical language (although not even the famous *Jesus* film uses biblical language throughout).

As well, the German school of higher criticism, starting in the late nineteenth century, wanted to divorce Christianity from its Jewish roots and make it more ethereal and ephemeral, as Jesus is depicted in *Jesus Christ, Superstar*, and *Godspell*, but that is not what Christians believe. Christians believe that the resurrection is where our hope resides, and the good news is that Jesus did die and resurrect for each and every person's failures, weaknesses, and sins, so that on Judgment Day, they will receive eternal life with Him.

It is important to recall the words of Gamaliel, a teacher of the law in the book of Acts, who advised the leaders of the Sanhedrin in their attempt to keep the apostles of Jesus Christ from preaching the good news: "Therefore, in the present case I advise you: Leave these men alone! Let them go! For, if their purpose or activity is of human origin, it will fail. But, if it is from God, you will not be able to stop these men; you will only find yourselves fighting against God" (Acts 5:38–39).

A faith grounded in the victory that Jesus won on the cross is not fearful of others, but is willing to be an ambassador of the good news of God's grace rather than an angry defender of the faith. In this way, Christianity overcame the Roman Empire—not by might, but by the testimony of the faithful, often as they were sent to their deaths by the pagan rulers of the state. In this way, by the time of Constantine, Rome had become Christianized.

So the resurrection of Jesus is important for us and for our children because it is through His death and resurrection that He forgave us and guaranteed the victory over sin and death once and for all.

FILM TO FAITH

Watch one or both of these movies:

- *The King of Kings* (1927)
- *Jesus*

Ask:

- How do *The King of Kings* and *Jesus* portray the resurrection of Jesus?
- How do these movies demonstrate the importance of the resurrection of Jesus?
- How does the resurrection of Jesus change your life?

Father, help me to be an ambassador of the good news of Jesus' resurrection, because it is through His death and resurrection that He forgave us and guaranteed the victory over sin and death.

LOOKING AHEAD

Would you like to be an amazing father or to be married to one? See the next devotion.

29

Courageous
Fatherhood

MOVIES THAT INSPIRE

Courageous
Father of the Bride (1991)

Would you like to be an amazing father or to be married to one?

Movies portraying men as great fathers are not all that common. *Courageous* was made just for that purpose. It tells the story of several policemen who are fathers and reveals some big mistakes. Following a major family tragedy, Adam (Alex Kendrick) assesses his failures as a father and seeks God's help in becoming better. His friends join in the journey.

The story is compelling. There's some great humor, as well as scenes you'll wish you'd had or will have with your children. In one, a father named Nathan (Ken Bevel) takes his daughter to dinner, gives her a ring, and tells her about his hopes for her happiness. In another, Adam makes a heartfelt apology to his son.

There is no better model of fatherhood than God Himself. In this day and age, a lot of children grow up with less-than-desirable father role models. The key to breaking this cycle is to look to God as Father. Consider 1 John 3:1: "See what great love the Father has lavished on us, that we should be called children of God! And that is what we are!" Imagine a human father with a never-ending store of the fruit of the Spirit just for you.

If you want to see a sweet and hilarious example of a father's love, watch *Father of the Bride*. In the 1991 version, Steve Martin plays George Banks, whose daughter Annie (Kimberly Williams) prepares for her wedding with his help and his money. There's lots of humor, but there are also some wonderful moments with a father and daughter showing deep appreciation for each other. And it provides some examples of how fun it can be to be a dad. In the end, it shows what a true blessing fatherhood is. Psalm 127:3 agrees: "Children are a heritage from the LORD, offspring a reward from him."

One of the best things about *Courageous* is that it demonstrates that God is in the business of helping you overcome mistakes. Several of the fathers in the movie were not good fathers, yet God wanted them to be good fathers and delighted in helping them when they became receptive.

God is in the redemption business. He wants to redeem marriages, parent/child relationships, communities, and industries (including the entertainment industry). He wants to bring more of heaven to all of society. In Matthew 6:9–10, Jesus taught his followers to pray, "Our Father in heaven, hallowed be your name, your kingdom come, your will be done, on earth as it is in heaven" (ESV). God wants more heaven on earth in our families, our communities, and our world. We move in the direction of redemption when we seek the guidance of the Holy Spirit.

Your Father in heaven will help you become a fantastic father on earth if you seek Him. Two of the greatest things you can experience in life are: 1) a close relationship to your Father God; and 2) a close father/child relationship. The more distant you are in either relationship, the more you miss in life.

One of the greatest lessons demonstrated in *Courageous* is the emotional reward for spending quality time with your children. You can't go back and get it for the years you miss. There are wonderful things to do and enjoy at all ages. Teenagers seldom enjoy hide-and-seek, but children at ages four and five love it.

My book *The Culture-Wise Family*, cowritten with Pat Boone, goes into detail about stages of cognitive development. Wise parents delight in fostering healthy development at every stage. There are simple things to do and things to avoid to make the best of each stage of development. Most are obvious if you ask God, "What's best for my children?"

FILM TO FAITH

Watch one or both of these movies:

- *Courageous*
- *Father of the Bride* (1991)

Ask:

- In *Courageous*, how did the fathers improve?
- Is tragedy necessary to trigger change?
- How can God help you to be a better father (or mother)?
- What kind of man would you like a daughter to marry?
- Are you raising your children to make wise choices?
- How do you love your children when you don't agree?

Father God, you are the ultimate model of fatherhood. Help me to live as your example for the world. Give me the grace to love my children unconditionally, without condoning what you've declared wrong. Make me a father who delights in his children like you delight in us.

LOOKING AHEAD

Do you want redemption? Do you like the movie or the book better? See the next devotion.

30

Reflections on Redemption

By Bruce Zachary[9]

MOVIES THAT INSPIRE

Ben-Hur (1959)

Saving Private Ryan (mature audiences)

Do you want redemption? Do you like the movie or the book better?

This isn't a review of actor Jason Statham's movie *Redemption* (which may or may not be pleasing to you), but it does have a cinematic and literary connection. I'm presently working my way through the American Film Institute's (AFI) top 100 list (2007 edition). Some other family members and I began with number 100 on that list, *Ben-Hur*, from 1959, and have worked down to number 15, *2001: A Space Odyssey*. One of the many blessings of cinema is the capacity to tell stories that move the heart, mind, and soul.

One of my favorite stories that has repeatedly been adapted to the big screen is *The Count of Monte Cristo* by Alexandre Dumas. In hardcover format, the book is a hefty 1,300-plus pages. Although I like to read, I have to admit that this book intimidates me. The movie, despite not being included in the AFI's top 100, allows me to enjoy one of the most epic redemption stories of all time.

---

9   Editor's note: Bruce Zachary is lead pastor of Calvary Nexus, the author of several books, and codirector of the Calvary Church Planting Network. He and his wife, Karen, live in Camarillo, California, with their sons Josh and Jonny.

I appreciate that there are certainly some of you literary aficionados who are smugly thinking, *The book is better*. Nevertheless, for countless viewers, great stories of drama, suspense, romance, and redemption are experienced on the big screen.

In the 1959 version of *Ben-Hur*, the importance of redemption in story is evident. Civil War General Lew Wallace wrote the book *Ben-Hur*, giving it the subtitle *A Tale of the Christ*. Yet in William Wyler's 1959 release, the face of Christ is never seen. This iconic redemption story will be famously remembered for the chariot race.

Even so, I will never forget the scene where Judah Ben-Hur (Charlton Heston) is dying of thirst on a forced march through the desert that is the Judean wilderness. All the other prisoners are given water, and as Judah cries out to God for deliverance, a hand extends a gourd filled with water to him.

A Roman soldier lifts his whip and declares, "I said no water for this one!" But as the soldier looks up, he presumably is looking into the face of Christ, and he lowers his whip and allows God's mercy to be shared with Judah. The direction and cinematography are remarkable, and redemption is playing out on many nuanced levels long before the chariot race.

The theme of redemption is found in a majority of the AFI's top 100. It is so universally attractive that it might seem we've been hardwired to resonate with redemptive stories, perhaps because "our story" might be part of some great and grand redemptive story. Two films included on the updated 2007 list (which weren't part of the original list published a decade earlier) are *The Shawshank Redemption* and *Saving Private Ryan* (coming in at #72 and #71 respectively).

These movies are iconic and the stories provocative. Watching Private Ryan reflect on whether the effort to rescue him and save his life was worth it. It has frequently moved me to contemplate whether Jesus' sacrifice for me was worth the sacrifice. I yearn to hear my Lord and Savior say, "Well done, good and faithful servant. … Enter into the joy of your lord" (Matthew 25:23 NKJV). I want to live my life in such a way that I don't waste the precious resources of time, talents, and treasure that God has entrusted to me. I want to ensure that my life was not wasted on selfish pursuits to the neglect of God.

It is the awareness of His redemption that motivates me. Prior to submitting my life to Jesus, I was in rebellion to the true and living God, despite being raised in an observant Jewish home. I share the blood of Abraham, Isaac, and Jacob, but it is only the blood of Jesus that can restore me in my relationship with God. It was His sacrifice that paid the price for my sin. And because he took the penalty that I deserve, I can experience a redeemed life with God. So my life is part of the greatest redemption story ever! The Bible is essentially a meta-redemptive epic.

Hollywood has handled Bible stories on numerous occasions. Some have done a better job than others in maintaining the theological details. It is undeniable that countless people have been exposed to God's redemptive story through the big screen. Even so, as a follower of Jesus, if you'll allow me, "I liked the book better."

FILM TO FAITH

Watch one or both of these movies:

- *Ben-Hur* (1959)
- *Saving Private Ryan* (mature audiences)

Ask:

- How does *Ben-Hur* show redemption?
- How does *Saving Private Ryan* show redemption?

- How is the story of redemption in the Bible better?
- How has redemption changed your life?

Father, make me keenly aware of your redemption of me, since it is only the blood of Jesus that can restore me in my relationship with you. Let me experience a redeemed life. Help me to see that my life is part of the greatest redemption story ever!

LOOKING AHEAD

Do you feel that your abundant, happy seasons pass too quickly and that the seasons of struggle, dryness, and outright suffering seem to drag? See the next devotion.

How Do I Smile in Adversity?

By Mary Driscoll[10]

MOVIES THAT INSPIRE
Life Is Beautiful
The Sound of Music

Do you feel that your abundant, happy seasons pass too quickly and that the seasons of struggle, dryness, and outright suffering seem to drag?

For everything there is a season. It does seem that the abundant, happy seasons pass quickly. Conversely, the seasons of struggle, dryness, and outright suffering seem to drag on too long. A day may feel like years. Children must still be cared for, and work must continue. Life goes on. As my wise Japanese friend used to say, "Life is fast, and time is short."

Our Christian faith calls us to joy and hope. But what if we don't feel hopeful or joyful? How do we smile in adversity?

Most people love movies where the hero or heroine overcomes personal struggle to find joy and happiness again. The 1997 Italian movie *Life Is Beautiful* is an example of how to push through adversity with joy. A Jewish-Italian man, Guido Orefice (Robert Benigni), and his son, Giosué (Giorgio Cantarini), are separated

---

10 Editor's note: Mary Driscoll analyzes Hollywood movie scripts and also writes inspirational articles for several publications.

from their wife and mother and sent to a concentration camp. Guido is determined to give his son a happy childhood experience by shielding him from the brutal reality of the camp, so he turns the horrors of the situation into an elaborate game.

Another movie that demonstrates the significance of joy in struggle is *The Sound of Music*. Maria (Julie Andrews) leaves the walls of the convent to govern the seven children of a hard-shelled, grieving widower. She captures every heart in that home with her winning attitude. Even when she's faced with the need to flee forever from Nazi-occupied Austria, she maintains her positive resolve. She is a pillar of strength for her new family. The audience is captivated as they watch Maria frolic in constant song, no matter what her circumstance.

What is it about these two movies that make all the difference? How do they live that kind of joy amid a deep sense of hopelessness? One of my favorite quotes in the Bible is "The joy of the LORD is your strength" (Nehemiah 9:10). In the darkest hours of life, it is important to remember that there is a light that will never be extinguished—the light of Jesus Christ. If I love a joyful God and He lives in me, then I must be joyful.

This is counterintuitive and includes some mystery, but if we look at the writings of the apostle Paul, we can see a certain surrender to inevitable types of suffering: "I am crucified with Christ: nevertheless, I live; yet not I, but Christ who liveth in me" (Galatians 2:20 KJV). The truth is that the resurrected Christ lives in each of us. If we truly believe, there is deep joy that envelopes our lives no matter what adversity may come our way.

The second aspect of the main characters in *Life Is Beautiful* and *The Sound of Music* is their care for others. They are both pillars of hope for those around them. Loving and caring for others takes us out of ourselves and our problems. This makes us more like Christ, who says, "This is my commandment, that you love one another as I have loved you" (John 15:12 ESV).

Whatever you may be facing, remember that God loves you with an everlasting love (Jeremiah 31:3).

FILM TO FAITH

Watch one or both of these movies:

- *Life Is Beautiful*
- *The Sound of Music*

Ask:

- How did the hero and heroine view the reality of their situation?
- What did they decide to do with their reality?
- What motivates the hero or heroine of the movie to act in a joyful way when they are faced with difficult and life-threatening circumstances?
- How can you take the negatives in your life and turn them into positives?
- How do you respond to God's love?

Lord, I come before you with my present struggles and my indifference to you and to others. I'm sorry if I have taken for granted all the blessings I have. Help me see those blessings and thank you for them. I give you my heart with all of its brokenness and confusion. I know you are the Healer who always gives us more than we could ever imagine. Help me know the depths of your love for me. In your name, Jesus. Amen.

LOOKING AHEAD

Do you wonder if anyone cares about you and your trials and tribulations? See the next devotion.

32

Does Anyone Really Care?

By Mary Driscoll

MOVIES THAT INSPIRE
Dunkirk (mature audiences)
The Blind Side (mature audiences)
Somebody Up There Likes Me

Do you wonder if anyone cares about you and your trials and tribulations?

Mother Teresa said that the greatest suffering in life is to be unwanted. Each one of us at some time or another feels unwanted. Society is obsessed with productivity, and it can make us feel like machines or robots. No one likes to be used. We are human *beings*, not human *doings*. So have you ever asked yourself, *Does anyone really care?* or *Who truly cares for me?*

We all love movies where characters show exceptional care for others. This inspires and encourages us to care more. For example, the 2017 movie *Dunkirk* is about a miraculous rescue of about three hundred and forty thousand soldiers who were stranded across the English Channel during World War II. Winston Churchill called on the average citizen to help their neighbors in need.

The true magic of the movie is that it focuses on the struggle and sacrifice of one man and his son to cross the dangerous channel, as it was under attack, in order to rescue soldiers. When they pick up a soldier with post-traumatic stress disorder who was shot down, the soldier does everything to convince them their rescue mission is a lost cause. He argues the problem is too massive and the danger too imminent and frightening for any one person to make a difference. Wanting to do something, they press on anyway.

Another movie that illustrates how one person who cares changes everything is *The Blind Side*. A wealthy Christian couple, Leigh Anne and Sean Tuohy (Sandra Bullock and Tim McGraw), from a diversity-deprived community, take in Michael Oher (Quinton Aaron), a homeless black teenager. Each of their lives is touched by the love and care they have found. With the help of his new family, Michael discovers his gifted ability to play football and becomes a star.

Many lives are transformed simply because someone cares. In the 1956 movie *Somebody Up There Likes Me*, Rocky Graziano (Paul Newman) illustrates this the best, as the winning line by the boxing champion is "Somebody up there likes me." Throughout the story, he sums up the philosophy of his life with the phrase, "Don't worry 'bout a thing!"

How do we fill the gap between wondering if anyone really cares and believing God cares deeply? Scripture tells us over and over that God cares. For example, "He will not allow your foot to slip; He who keeps you will not slumber" (Psalm 121:3 NASB), and "So he got up and came to his father. But while he was still a long way off, his father saw him and felt compassion for him, and ran and embraced him and kissed him" (Luke 15:20 NASB), part of a parable describing God's love for those who have forsaken Him.

In fact, there are 550 instances of *care* in the Bible. It seems God not only goes out of His way to convince us that He cares for each and every person, but He also asks each of us to care for one another. Once we accept this truth of God's love for us, we must do the same for others. Jesus is quite serious as He instructs us how to treat our neighbors: "A new commandment I give to you, that you love one another, even as I have loved you, that you also love one another. By this all men will know that you are My disciples, if you have love for one another" (John 13:34–35 NASB).

Sometimes it's hard to know what comes first, the chicken or the egg. There's a definite connection between God's love and care for us personally and our love for others. This is best summed up in 1 Peter 4:8: "Above all, love each other deeply, because love covers over a multitude of sins." Once our sins are covered, the veil is lifted, and we discover more and more love. Therefore, sometimes we must love and care for others before we can clearly recognize God's love and care for us.

FILM TO FAITH

Watch one or more of these movies:

- *Dunkirk* (mature audiences)
- *The Blind Side* (mature audiences)
- *Somebody Up There Likes Me* (1956)

Ask:

- What made the heroes feel alone or forgotten?
- What type of trouble did the thoughts or the actual reality of being alone and unloved cause?
- How did the heroes act when they thought no one cared for them?
- What happened to the hero once he understood he was loved?
- Have you ever felt unloved or forgotten by everyone?
- How have you felt that someone cared for you?

Father, I often fail to notice your loving care for me. Amid the noise and stress of life, help me take time to remember that you have counted every hair on my head and I am your child. Keep me close to your heart and impress on me that I'm never alone. Help me to see you more clearly in others by recognizing that whatever I do to the least of your people, I do to you. In times when I feel alone, let me speak your words, "The Lord is my shepherd, I shall not want." In Jesus' name, I pray.

LOOKING AHEAD

Am I really alone? Why do I feel lonely? Can any good come from the feeling of loneliness? See the next devotion.

33

Am I Alone?

By Mary Driscoll

MOVIES THAT INSPIRE

The Last Holiday (mature audiences)
The Miracle Worker

Many of us are swept up in our fast-paced culture. Focusing on productivity and appearances, we constantly keep busy. Moments of silence are rare and can be frightening because there seems to be loneliness in silence. This is a great time to ask yourself, *Am I really alone? Why do I feel lonely?* and *Can any good come from the feeling of loneliness?* As difficult as these questions may be, they can launch you into the best prayer time possible.

Two movies that deal with issues of loneliness, both directly and indirectly, are *The Last Holiday* and *The Miracle Worker*. In *The Last Holiday*, Georgia Byrd (Queen Latifah) is an introvert who has spent her life alone. When she finds out she has a terminal illness, the news takes her in a whole new direction, as she withdraws her entire life savings and goes on the adventure of a lifetime.

The Miracle Worker recounts the true story of Annie Sullivan (Anne Bancroft) and Helen Keller (Patty Duke). Helen suffers from isolation and loneliness due to an inability to see, hear, or speak, to the degree that she acts out in an uncivilized and violent manner. As Helen is on the brink of being institutionalized, Annie must break free from her own lonely and troubled past to help Helen communicate and discover she's not alone.

Does God have anything to say about loneliness? Could He possibly care in such a detailed way about our feelings?

When we look at Scripture, we see that we have a very personal, caring God. After Jesus was resurrected, observe the last words given to us through His disciples: "Then Jesus came up and spoke to them, saying, 'All authority has been given to Me in heaven and on earth. Go therefore and make disciples of all the nations, baptizing them in the name of the Father and the Son and the Holy Spirit, teaching them to observe all that I commanded you; and lo, I am with you always, even to the end of the age'" (Matthew 28:18–20 NASB).

This passage makes it clear that Jesus Christ is always near. Also notice that Jesus doesn't just give us orders and then leave, even though He is God and we should gladly accept that as well. First, He approaches or comes near. This implies that He is personally concerned about our feelings, because in this passage He sees that the disciples are doubtful and maybe a little scared. He comes closer because He is concerned about how they feel. Then He assures them that *He* has all authority. He's our God who blesses us, strengthens us, and instructs us, and then He tells us not to worry because He is *always* with us. What more could we ask?

God allows us to feel inadequate, scared, lonely, and doubtful so that He can approach us. This is what prayer is, a conversation with the One who cares about you and me the most. If we look back on our lives, we will see that our greatest tribulations or trials were followed by our greatest blessings from God when we turned to Him.

At different times in my life, each of my four children has faced a life-threatening situation, due to an illness, accident, or allergic reaction to food. There is nothing that brings us to our knees faster than holding our suffering children in our arms. And nothing moves heaven more than this kind of plea.

At these moments, we know we are not alone. That is why we reach out to our God who cares, who comes near us to heal and restore.

FILM TO FAITH

Watch one or both of these movies:

- *The Last Holiday* (mature audiences)
- *The Miracle Worker*

Ask:

- What circumstances led the main characters in these movies to feel alone?
- What effects did loneliness have on their lives?
- How did the characters view God's role in the circumstances of their lives?
- In *The Last Holiday*, what did Georgia Byrd learn about God's plans for her life?
- In *The Miracle Worker*, how did Annie challenge the idea that Helen was deaf, dumb, and blind because she was cursed by God?
- What did the lead characters in each movie do with the challenge and/or tragedy they faced?
- How has God shown up in your life when you needed Him or even when you least expected Him to show up?

Father, help me to remember you are with me always. When I'm feeling lonely, remind me not to be afraid and to see it as a call to spend time in prayer with you, the One who cares and loves me the most. I give to you all of my doubts and troubles and ask you to come near me to bless me, strengthen me, instruct me, and send me out to do your will. Keep close to me your words, "I alone know the plans I have for you, plans to bring you prosperity and not disaster, plans to bring about the future you hope for." I ask this in Jesus' name, amen.

LOOKING AHEAD

Why do bad things happen to nice people? See the next devotion.

34

Why Do Bad Things Happen to Nice People?

MOVIES THAT INSPIRE

The Gospel According to Matthew aka *The Visual Bible: Matthew* (1993)

The Velveteen Rabbit (2009)

Why do bad things happen to nice people?

The question is not *Why do bad things happen to* good *people?* because the Bible makes it clear that "There is no one righteous, not even one" (Romans 3:10) and "No one is good—except God alone" (Mark 10:18). Even so, why do bad things happen to you and me when we're trying to do the right thing? And why do bad things happen to babies and others who don't deserve such pain and suffering?

As many theologians note, the Bible indicates there are four reasons that bad things happen to people: the world, the flesh, the devil, and God's training of us.

The first reason is the world. We live in a world that has laws designed into it. If a tsunami or earthquake comes and hurts a baby, it's not a personal attack; it's just part of the world. Most problems come because we live in the world governed by God's created and ordained natural laws. If a bus skids on a road because of ice, it may not be the driver's fault or the ice's fault or God's fault. It's how creation operates.

The second reason is the flesh. For a lot of people, the flesh is what takes them out because they're constantly submitting to its desires. Mayors, politicians, and businesspeople are often in the news because they succumb to greed, lust, gluttony, or another temptation of the flesh.

The third reason is the devil, who has less to do with it since the first two reasons cover most of the problems we face. And the fourth reason is God directly working on us, which usually happens with only a few people who are on a mission from God.

The Bible shows that Jesus experienced all four of these reasons but didn't succumb to any of them. For instance, when the devil tempted Jesus in Matthew 4:1–11:

> Then Jesus was led up by the Spirit into the wilderness to be tempted by the devil. He fasted forty days and forty nights, and afterwards he was famished. The tempter came and said to him, "If you are the Son of God, command these stones to become loaves of bread." But he answered, "It is written, 'One does not live by bread alone, but by every word that comes from the mouth of God.'" Then the devil took him to the holy city and placed him on the pinnacle of the temple, saying to him, "If you are the Son of God, throw yourself down; for it is written, 'He will command his angels concerning you,' and 'On their hands they will bear you up, so that you will not dash your foot against a stone.'" Jesus said to him, "Again it is written, 'Do not put the Lord your God to the test.'" Again, the devil took him to a very high mountain and showed him all the kingdoms of the world and their splendor; and he said to him, "All these I will give you, if you will fall down and worship me." Jesus said to him, "Away with you, Satan! for it is written, 'Worship the Lord your God, and serve only him.'" Then

the devil left him, and suddenly angels came and waited on him (NRSV).

The word-for-word movie rendition of this passage from Matthew is portrayed powerfully in *The Gospel According to Matthew* (1993) also known as *The Visual Bible: Matthew*. Of course, even though Jesus is fully God and fully man, He was led by the Holy Spirit, so He is being disciplined, and all four reasons can be seen in the passage.

The good news is that God "comforts us in all our troubles, so that we can comfort those in any trouble with the comfort we ourselves receive from God" (2 Corinthians 1:4). Our job in life is not just making widgets and gadgets; the most important thing we can do is to learn to be compassionate, to have empathy for others, to have a deepening of wisdom, to bring joy to others, and to have the image of God. Trials and tribulations are not a sidetrack; the sidetrack is our getting so egocentric that we forget there are higher responsibilities.

The truth is, we're not made to live forever. We're made to wear out. Those of us who are saved live in the world of the dying, headed to the world of the living. Like the Velveteen Rabbit who became tattered from being loved, we aren't questioning if we are going to die; we're asking what we do on the road to the other side as we lose our hair.

Why do bad things happen to you and me? Perhaps so we learn to really love and comfort others, because the more we do so, the more joy we have.

FILM TO FAITH

Watch one or both of these movies:

- *The Gospel According to Matthew* aka *The Visual Bible: Matthew* (1993)

- *The Velveteen Rabbit* (2009)

Ask:

- How does the temptation of Jesus in *The Gospel According to Matthew* show you why bad things happen to nice people?
- How does *The Velveteen Rabbit* show that we face trials and tribulations to comfort and love others?
- How has God helped you face and overcome "bad things"?
- How have you comforted others with the comfort you received from God when bad things happened?

Father, please save me, rescue me, help me, and comfort me when I face bad things, such as trials and tribulations, and help me to comfort others with the comfort I receive from you. In Jesus Christ's holy name, amen.

LOOKING AHEAD

Why are relationships so difficult? Why do I argue with those I love? See the next devotion.

35

Why Are Relationships So Difficult?

MOVIES THAT INSPIRE
WALL-E
Rocky Balboa (mature audiences)

Why are relationships so difficult? Why do I argue with those I love?

Proverbs 27:17 helps answer that question: "As iron sharpens iron, so one person sharpens another."

A minister friend of mine once was counseling a couple at their home. The husband had recently been diagnosed with multiple sclerosis, and they also had suffered economic tragedy when he lost his government job as a result. During one of the counseling sessions, there was this awful grinding noise in the background: their son's rock polisher.

My friend asked if the parents could have him turn it off, so they could discuss the problems they were facing. When they said that the machine had to be left running, he asked them to show him the machine. They took him to the polisher, which looked like a small vertical cement mixer with a funnel, a belly, and three gears at the bottom.

The parents told my friend that rocks found in a pond or stream are put into the machine. If they're precious or semi-precious, they'll polish; if they're not, they'll be ground to dirt. He asked, "How do they polish?" and the husband explained, "All the gears do is throw the rocks up in the air, and the rocks polish by hitting against each other."

Hoping that the family would turn it off, my friend questioned, "How long does it take?" "The more precious they are," the husband explained, "the longer they take to polish." So my friend dug deeper: "Well, how do you know when it's finished?" The wife replied, "When you can take the polished gemstone out of the polisher and see your face in it."

My friend used the rock polisher as an example to help the family. He told them that they were like the gemstones. The losses of the husband's health and his job were battering them against each other, and if they were precious, they would polish. God would know when they were polished—when He could see His face and likeness in them.

Every human being wants to be their own lord and savior and control their own life. Yet we know that we don't control much of our life, and even when we think we're controlling it, we're not. One way we try to do that is to get away from people, but in God's system, our relationships and situations polish us.

Many romantic movies and comedies demonstrate growth through conflict. In *WALL-E*, WALL-E and Eve are often in conflict. Each funny little contention and altercation produces growth in them. Eventually, Eve discovers she needs WALL-E, and WALL-E has to rescue Eve.

In *Rocky Balboa*, Rocky (Sylvester Stallone) is past his prime boxing days. His son, Robert, disagrees with him often. Robert is an up-and-coming corporate executive who looks down on his father in many ways, but they slowly come to appreciate and love the other. When Robert tells Rocky not to fight again, Rocky gives him some profound advice about success in life: "It ain't about how hard you're hit, it's about how you can get hit and keep moving forward."[11] Rocky concludes that blaming others won't help Robert. They are iron sharpening iron, polishing each other. They become a great father-and-son team.

Our church, our family, and our coworkers, for instance, are our rock polishers. The circumstances of sickness, disease, or poverty are the gears that throw us up in the air and force us to hit against each other. If we abandon each other—if we abandon people, if we abandon coming together—we don't get polished. We get polished by knocking off the imperfections and rough edges of each other. So we need each other to be polished. Look forward to God seeing His face reflected in your polished character.

FILM TO FAITH

Watch one or both of these movies:

- *WALL-E*
- *Rocky Balboa* (mature audiences)

Ask:

- How do Eve and WALL-E polish each other?
- How do Eve and WALL-E become reflections of God's image?
- How do Rocky and Robert polish each other?
- How do Rocky and Robert become reflections of God's image?
- Who has helped polish you to reflect God's image?

Father, help me to love my wife, children, family, and friends, and to become so polished that you will see your

---

11 *Rocky Balboa*, IMDb, accessed September 26, 2017, http://www.imdb.com/title /tt0479143/.

image in me—the image of your love, joy, peace, patience,
kindness, goodness, faith, gentleness, and self-control. In
Jesus' name, amen.

LOOKING AHEAD

Do you believe that what God wants for you is better than what
you want for yourself? See the next devotion.

The Rewards
of Repentance

MOVIES THAT INSPIRE
Flywheel
Sergeant York

Do you believe that what God wants for you is better than what you want for yourself?

In both *Flywheel* and *Sergeant York*, the main characters are eking out a miserable existence and are on the verge of catastrophe when they repent and fully give their lives to God. The first things they are called to do are radical but lead to tremendous blessings.

One difference between *Flywheel* and *Sergeant York* is that *Sergeant York* features a major Hollywood star, Gary Cooper, and was the top box office hit of 1941. It trounced the competition. Cooper won the best actor Oscar playing Sergeant York. On the opposite end of the spectrum, *Flywheel* was the first movie made by the Kendrick Brothers (*Facing the Giants*, *Fireproof*, *Courageous*, and *War Room*) and was about as low-budget as a movie could be, but the story is better than most Hollywood blockbusters.

In *Flywheel*, Jay Austin (Alex Kendrick) is a churchgoing used-car dealer who takes advantage of customers. He even takes advantage of a pastor who prays that God will bless him the way he was blessed by the "deal." Jay knows his pastor was not blessed by the deal, and this leads to radical repentance.

Jay gets right with God, then goes and pays back those he believes he gave a bad deal. I won't spoil the movie for you, but his radical transformation leads to tremendous blessing, not just in his business but also in his family and in his conscience. You live in far greater peace when you trust God and do as He directs.

Sergeant York is based on a true story. In the movie, Alvin York (Gary Cooper) is a heavy drinker on his way to shoot someone to death when lightning strikes and destroys his rifle. He experiences such a radical transformation that he becomes a sober, conscientious objector in World War I; he doesn't want to use a gun to kill anyone. God has him visit the man he was previously going to kill and treat him with kindness. It's a great scene. There's also a wonderful scene where York, the conscientious objector, shows he can shoot a rifle better than anyone else in the army.

Eventually, he's sent home to pray about his role as a soldier. Atop a mountain with his trusty hunting dog, York receives a divine message from the Word of God to "render unto Caesar the things that are Caesar's." In a fierce battle in France, his superior officer dies, and he winds up responsible for leading the few remaining men in his outfit. He has them do their best to stay down and goes off to knock out the machine guns killing his friends. He and his handful of men wind up taking 132 prisoners, and later he's awarded the Medal of Honor.

In these movies, the heroes model 2 Corinthians 5:17: "If anyone is in Christ, the new creation has come: The old has gone, the new is here!"

You can attend church like Jay Austin and not experience "the new." It's when you give God control of your life that you experience the new. With it comes the fruit of the Spirit. These fruits are a tremendous blessing to you, and they make you a tremendous blessing to others. When you spend your day walking in the guidance of the Holy Spirit, you spend your nights sleeping peacefully with a clear conscience.

Consider the leading of the Holy Spirit when you're looking for opportunities to be entertained, be it television, movies, or music. Radical Christian living is not just how you feel about guns or car sales, it's about all of life.

What you eat, what you watch, and what you say can all be directed by the Holy Spirit to make you more like Jesus. And the more you're like Jesus, the greater the blessing you'll be to others. As Jesus says, "Come to me, all you who are weary and burdened, and I will give you rest. Take my yoke upon you and learn from me, for I am gentle and humble in heart, and you will find rest for your souls. For my yoke is easy and my burden is light" (Matthew 11:28–30).

Following the leading of the Holy Spirit brings rest for your soul. It's when we part from God's ways that our lives are much more disturbed.

FILM TO FAITH

Watch one or both of these movies:

- *Flywheel*
- *Sergeant York*

Ask:

- Was Jay Austin a Christian by just attending church?
- How was Jay Austin happier after his radical transformation?
- How was Sergeant York happier after he was transformed?

- o What does God direct you to do?
- o Is there anything in your life in need of radical transformation?

Father, I thank you that what you desire for me is much better than what I desire for myself. Help me to do whatever you desire, no matter how radical it may appear. I turn my life over to you. In Jesus' name, amen.

LOOKING AHEAD

Have you experienced love, betrayal, and the ultimate vindication, or all three? See the next devotion.

God Is in Control

By Jaime Loya[12]

MOVIE THAT INSPIRES:
The Count of Monte Cristo (2002)

Have you experienced love, betrayal, and the ultimate vindication, or all three?

One of my favorite movies has to be the 2002 version of the famous novel *The Count of Monte Cristo*. It's a story of love, betrayal, and the ultimate vindication. As human beings, it is possible that we will experience at least one, if not all three, sometime in our life.

In *The Count of Monte Cristo*, Edmond Dantes (Jim Caviezel) has been betrayed by his best friend, Fernand Mondego (Guy Pearce). Although he's innocent, Edmond is sent to the Chateau d'If, one of the worst prisons at the time. After years of pain and suffering, Edmond's life is interrupted by another prisoner he affectionately calls Priest, an elderly gentleman who teaches him math, science, economics, and the art of war in return for Edmond's help in escaping.

However, the tunnel collapses on top of the old man while they are escaping, and he soon dies. Before his last breath, Priest tells Edmond the secret location of a hidden treasure known as the Lost Treasure of Spada. Edmond goes in search of it. The legend

---

12 Editor's note: Jaime Loya is the founder and lead pastor of Cross Church in San Benito, Texas. He is a committed follower of Jesus Christ, a loving husband, and a devoted father of four amazing children.

of the lost treasure turns out to be true, and Edmond becomes one of the richest men in the world, but instead of thanking God for his good fortune, he is bent on seeking revenge. Watch the movie to see the ending.

This story reminds me of the story of Joseph, which begins in Genesis 37:3–5:

> Now Israel loved Joseph more than any of his other sons, because he had been born to him in his old age; and he made an ornate robe for him. When his brothers saw that their father loved him more than any of them, they hated him and could not speak a kind word to him. Joseph had a dream, and when he told it to his brothers, they hated him all the more.

How sad that someone would hate you because of your dream. (Keep in mind that not everybody is for you, and not everyone who is your friend on Facebook is your friend for real.) Joseph's brothers threw him into a pit and later sold him as a slave. They told their father that a wild animal killed Joseph, and as far as they were concerned, Joseph was dead and gone.

By divine providence, Joseph ended up in Egypt. There, he was sold to Potiphar only to be later falsely accused of rape by Potiphar's wife. He ended up in prison for life, similar to what happened to Edmond Dantes.

After many years, Joseph was miraculously delivered from prison because of his God-given ability to interpret dreams (he correctly interpreted Pharaoh's dream). Because of this, Joseph was made second-in-command over all of Egypt. Within twenty-four hours, Joseph went from rotting in prison to being the second-most-powerful man in the world.

Later, Joseph got his chance for revenge. His long-lost brothers showed up at his doorstep begging for food because of the famine ravaging the entire land. Instead of taking revenge, Joseph had mercy on them. He realized that everything that had happened to him, including his misfortunes, was used by God to bring him to this strategic position in life.

Joseph is quoted in Genesis 50:19–21 telling his brothers, "Don't be afraid. Am I in the place of God? You intended to harm me, but God intended it for good to accomplish what is now being done, the saving of many lives. So then, don't be afraid. I will provide for you and your children."

How many of us could have done that? Joseph was convinced that although people meant to harm him, God protected him and ultimately used it for his good. Joseph could have taken vengeance on his brothers, but he chose to give them the gift of forgiveness.

God wants us to trust Him. He knows what He is doing and why things happen the way they do. We are not called to understand but to have faith in a God who loves us and cares for us.

There may be people whom God is calling you to forgive. You may have a family member or close friend in your life who betrayed you or hurt you. You will never enjoy your future holding on to your past. It's time to let go and let God handle it.

FILM TO FAITH

Watch this movie:

- *The Count of Monte Cristo* (2002)

Ask:

- How would you feel if what happened to Edmond happened to you?
- What about Joseph? What would you have done in his case?

- What similarities do you find between the movie and the story of Joseph?
- Why do you think forgiveness is so hard?
- How is God asking you to simply trust Him?

Dear heavenly Father, I know I don't know everything. I don't always know your plan or see the purpose. I know you are asking me to trust you in everything that I am going through, and I want you to know that I do. I choose to trust you in everything. If that means forgiving, then I will forgive. If that means waiting, then I will wait. If that means to just be still, then I will be still and know that you are God. I pray this in the holy name of Jesus, amen.

LOOKING AHEAD

If the world will never know our name, how we can still make a difference? See the next devotion.

All in Due Time

By Jaime Loya

Hidden Figures (mature audiences)

If the world will never know our name, how we can still make a difference?

Hidden Figures is based on a true story from the 1960s, when the United States raced against Russia to see who could put a man in space first. Three brilliant, African-American women working at NASA, Katherine Johnson, Dorothy Vaughan, and Mary Jackson (Taraji Henson, Octavia Spencer, and Janelle Monáe), served as the brains who launched the first astronaut, John Glenn, into orbit. It was a seemingly impossible task made possible by three amazing women.

It wasn't until the movie released that we discovered how significant these women were in the space program. Not all people of significance are remembered, and not everybody who plays an important part in history will have a movie made in their honor. The world may never know our name, but we can still make a difference where we are and with those closest to us.

Scripture includes an obscure person who is included among the greatest people of faith who ever lived. Hebrews 11 contains the names and accomplishments of many significant characters in the Bible—people like Moses, Abraham, King David, and others. But verse 32 adds an unfamiliar name: "And what shall I more say?

I do not have time to tell of Gideon, Barak, Samson and Jephthah, about David and Samuel, and the prophets."

Some of these names are more familiar than others. We hear about David all the time, but when was the last time you heard about Jephthah? That name may not mean much to us, but it meant a lot to the people God used him to deliver. Judges 11:1–11 says:

Now Jephthah the Gileadite was a mighty warrior, but he was the son of a prostitute. Gilead was the father of Jephthah. And Gilead's wife also bore him sons. And when his wife's sons grew up, they drove Jephthah out and said to him, 'You shall not have an inheritance in our father's house, for you are the son of another woman.' Then Jephthah fled from his brothers and lived in the land of Tob, and worthless fellows collected around Jephthah and went out with him. After a time the Ammonites made war against Israel. And when the Ammonites made war against Israel, the elders of Gilead went to bring Jephthah from the land of Tob. And they said to Jephthah, 'Come and be our leader that we may fight against the Ammonites.' But Jephthah said to the elders of Gilead, 'Did you not hate me and drive me out of my father's house? Why have you come to me now when you are in distress?' And the elders of Gilead said to Jephthah, 'That is why we have turned to you now, that you may go with us and fight against the Ammonites and be our head over all the inhabitants of Gilead.' Jephthah said to the elders of Gilead, 'If you bring me home again to fight against the Ammonites, and the LORD gives them over to me, I will be your head.' And the elders of Gilead said to Jephthah, 'The LORD will be witness between us, if we do not do as you say.' So Jephthah went with the elders of Gilead, and the people made him head and leader over them." (ESV)

What an amazing story of this hidden figure in the Bible. Jephthah teaches us that we don't have to be famous to make a difference. He was born of an adulterous affair his father had with a prostitute and was cast out of his house. For years, he lived in obscurity and rejection, but the time came when he was needed. This was his due season. Galatians 6:9 says, "And let us not grow weary of doing good, for in due season we will reap, if we do not give up" (ESV).

In life, it doesn't matter where we start but rather where we finish. God will often use unqualified people to do uncommon things. One of my favorite quotes from *Hidden Figures* was said by Mary Jackson: "Every time we get a chance to get ahead, they move the finish line."[13] Sometimes it feels like we're not getting very far or getting the credit we deserve, but the time will come when the world will need us and take notice, just as God took Jephthah from obscurity and placed him over the entire nation. As Psalm 27:10 says, "When my father and my mother forsake me, then the LORD will take me up" (KJV).

If God could do it for Jephthah, he can do it for you—all in due time!

FILM TO FAITH

Watch this movie:

- *Hidden Figures* (mature audiences)

---

13 *Hidden Figures*, *IMDb*, accessed September 26, 2017, http://www.imdb.com/title/tt4846340/.

Ask:

- What about *Hidden Figures* impacts you the most?
- What about Jephthah's story impacts you the most?
- Have you ever felt overlooked or unappreciated? What happened?
- Is there someone you may need to recognize? If so, who and why?
- How can you trust that God will make a way for you?

Dear Lord, I will continue to patiently wait for you. I know that things may not happen on my time but when the time is right. I trust that you see all, hear all, and know all. I will not fret or be anxious, knowing my time will come. When it does, I will be ready and vow to give you all the glory. In the precious name of Jesus, amen.

LOOKING AHEAD

Have you ever wished you could be rich? See the next devotion.

39

The Wonders and Hazards of Wealth

MOVIES THAT INSPIRE
Citizen Kane
It Happened One Night

Have you ever wished you could be rich?

Much of the good done in the world is accomplished by people rich enough to give money to good causes. Virtually every church and all missions receive much of their income from their most wealthy contributors, and the many government programs for the poor are largely funded by taxes paid by the rich. Being rich is not evil, but it has hazards, and the movies *Citizen Kane* and *It Happened One Night* offer great lessons on the subject. They're worth watching and discussing.

In *Citizen Kane*, Charles Foster Kane (Orson Welles) is a man whose family came into great wealth when he was a child. Upon receiving trust fund money, he enters the newspaper business and experiences great success with yellow journalism (scandalous news). He gains both wealth and power and marries the niece of the president, but his life spirals downward when he gets involved in an affair.

All his wealth can't clean up the mess he's made of his life. He winds up very lonely in a huge mansion called Xanadu. His dying word is *Rosebud*. At the end, the movie reveals the secret of Rosebud, but the reporter who failed to discover it says that no one word can sum up a man's entire life.

Indeed, the message of the movie is that Citizen Kane was a complicated man whose life was full of many different reflections. That said, it becomes clear that the thing Kane longed for the most was not the wealth and fame he garnered during his life, but the love and family that he lost.

As mentioned, wealth can be a great blessing to those who become wealthy and those who are helped by funds given by the rich, but with wealth comes all sorts of problems. Several are shown in the 1934 Best Picture Oscar winner, a delightful comedy titled *It Happened One Night*.

In the story, Ellie Andrews (Claudette Colbert) is the wealthy daughter of Alexander Andrews (Walter Connolly). She elopes with a young man interested in marrying into wealth, and her father wants the marriage annulled. Being a spoiled brat, Ellie runs away. Her father uses his wealth and power to have her hunted down, and a recently fired journalist, Peter Warne (Clark Gable), offers to help her escape in exchange for an exclusive on her story. The movie shows how Ellie is out of touch with the real world and how she has trouble being appreciated as anything more than an opportunity to get some of her money.

Can you imagine how many people would come asking you for money if the world knew you had three billion dollars? Even if you are an exemplary person, great wealth can make you a target of both good and evil people. There are temptations the rich experience that the poor don't face. The greatest may be that pursuing wealth can become more important than pursuing God, as Jesus tells us in Matthew 6:24: "No one can serve two masters. Either you will hate the one and love the other, or you will be devoted to the one and despise the other. You cannot serve both God and money."

On the bright side, pursuing God can lead to tremendous financial prosperity. Proverbs 8:17–21 tells of the benefits of pursuing wisdom: "I love those who love me, and those who seek me find me. With me are riches and honor, enduring wealth and prosperity. My fruit is better than fine gold; what I yield surpasses choice silver. I walk in the way of righteousness, along the paths of justice, bestowing a rich inheritance on those who love me and making their treasuries full."

Notice that pursuing God brings wealth with righteousness and justice. Pursuing God brings fruit better than gold. That fruit is the fruit of the Spirit—love, joy, peace, patience, kindness, goodness, faithfulness, gentleness, and self-control. With these, the possession of great wealth is a blessing. God can direct a humble heart in how to use it. It is *not* His desire that everyone lives in poverty. His desire is prosperity, but true prosperity values the fruit of the Spirit far above the amount of one's financial wealth.

It Happened One Night ends on a high note with Ellie finally being appreciated for something greater than just being a rich girl: she finds a man who loves her for herself rather than for her money. *Citizen Kane* ends by showing the longing Charles Foster Kane had for the joy, love, and family he knew before wealth and power became his obsession. Of course, the joy and love he really needs—and we need—is the joy and love that come from a right relationship to God.

FILM TO FAITH

Watch one or both of these movies:

- *Citizen Kane*
- *It Happened One Night*

Ask:

- What made Charles Foster Kane truly happy: sledding as a child or great wealth and power?
- What were Charles Foster Kane's greatest mistakes?
- What made Ellie Andrews happy?
- How would you feel if people only wanted to be with you because you have money?
- How do you put God first and handle money now, and if you were to gain great wealth?

Father, I thank you for your generosity. Help me to always consider the fruit of the Spirit more valuable than money, but never to think of money itself as evil.

LOOKING AHEAD

Do you want the freedom to be loved by and to love God? See the next devotion.

40

Stand Up for God!

MOVIE THAT INSPIRES
For Greater Glory (mature audiences)

Do you want the freedom to be loved by and to love God? Do you want the freedom to manifest the fruit of the Spirit?

Religious freedom is the very cornerstone of all our other freedoms. President James Madison defined religion as "the duty we owe to our Creator,"[14] which is to know God and to make Him known.

Vladimir Lenin believed that if he could control the mass media, he could control the world. Under the guidance of Lenin and the total control of the 1917 communist revolution, two-thirds of all churches in Russia were torn down, and 60 to 120 million people were killed. The atheistic communists succeeded in Russia because the people had forgotten God. Joseph Stalin, Lenin's successor, wanted to undermine America's morality, patriotism, and spiritual life.

Why do atheists want the Bible out of schools? Because it's powerful. It is often alleged that most people who come to Christ do so out of reading the Bible. We need to rebuild our country's patriotism, our morality, and our spiritual life—the very things that Stalin wanted to tear down. We're going to have to do that by rebuilding our foundation on God.

---

14 "Madison's Amendments to the Declaration of Rights, [29 May–12 June 1776]," *Founders Online*, accessed September 28, 2017, https://founders.archives.gov/documents/Madison/01-01-02-0054-0003.

What is the foundation of the U.S. Constitution? The Declaration of Independence. What is the foundation of the Declaration of Independence? It's mentioned at the very beginning of the document: "We hold these truths to be self-evident, that all men are created equal, that they are endowed by their Creator with certain unalienable Rights, that among these are Life, Liberty and the pursuit of Happiness."

Jesus loves us. He paid the ultimate price to rescue us from evil. No king or president can take that away from us. Our rights don't come from the government. They don't come from the state or the will of the elite in the media. They come from God, and if we forget God, then the people in power are going to be corrupted by their power, just as Lenin and Stalin were.

Power knows no limits. For example, King Ahab and Queen Jezebel believed they could simply steal Naboth's land and kill him, but they suffered the ultimate judgment for their greed (see 1 Kings 21). The good news about the United States is that the Constitution protects us. "Thou shalt not steal" protects the little guy from being imposed upon by the government. And the ultimate protection is from the Bill of Rights—that Congress shall make no law respecting the establishment of religion, or prohibiting the free exercise of it.

Did you watch the 2012 movie *For Greater Glory*? In Mexico in the 1920s, the priests, ministers, and Christians stood up. They did this because the priests were being killed and the churches were being defamed. They faced off with the forces of darkness and stopped the socialistic, atheistic dictator from doing the dirty deed of killing religion in Mexico. At the end, they cry, "Viva Cristo Rey!" ("Long live Christ the King!").

Likewise, if we stand up, filled with His Spirit, the gates of hell will not prevail. God will empower us, and we will have the power to take every thought captive for Jesus.

Remember Saint Telemachus. In AD 404, at the heart of the gladiatorial games in Rome when the authorities were killing Christians in vile ways, Telemachus was a Christian in the most remote region of Europe. Called by God, he walked miles to Rome to the games. He was shocked at the maiming, the killing, and the murder, and yelled, "Stop, in the name of Jesus Christ!" Then this Christian jumped into the arena in the Coliseum and repeated, "Stop, in the name of Jesus Christ!" As a gladiator killed him, his frail body fell, and his blood was poured out in the Coliseum, he looked up at the Roman emperor and said, "Stop, in the name of Jesus Christ!" There never was another gladiatorial game in the Coliseum.

Think about it. One man against the whole Roman Empire.

You and every person of faith can be a Telemachus. Every person can walk through life in the victory of Viva Cristo Rey. Every person can stand up against the encroachment of our rights. So jump into the arena and say, "Stop, in the name of Jesus Christ!"

FILM TO FAITH

Watch this movie:

- *For Greater Glory* (mature audiences)

Ask:

- How does *For Greater Glory* show the humanistic attack on religious freedom?
- How does the young boy, José, stand up for his freedom to love God and his neighbor?
- How did the Christians stand up for their religious freedom?
- How have you stood up for Jesus Christ?

Father, I love you so much that I want to be free to worship you in word and in deed. So please inspire me and empower me to stand up for Jesus Christ and for the religious freedom to do so, in Jesus Christ's name by the power of the Holy Spirit, amen.

LOOKING AHEAD

Do you want to be totally surrendered to God so His will will be done? See the next devotion.

41

Lift Up Your Hands

MOVIE THAT INSPIRES
Rio Grande Ranger

Do you ever lift up your hands in church or other times in prayer and praise? Do you want to be totally surrendered to God so His will will be done?

My father was a Hollywood movie star starting in the 1930s and then a star in Broadway theatre after World War II. At the beginning of his career, he had a Hollywood Western movie series called *The Texas Rangers*, starring Bob "Tex" Allen. When he arrested the villains in these movies, such as in *Rio Grande Ranger*, the bad guys lifted their hands to show they had dropped their guns and surrendered.

Lifting up your hands to surrender did not start in Hollywood movies. There are over twenty-eight verses in the Bible about lifting up hands in surrender, prayer, blessing, or supplication. The apostle Paul says in 1 Timothy 2:8, "Therefore, I want the men in every place to pray, lifting up holy hands, without wrath and dissension" (NASB). In the Bible, the gesture is often a sign of surrender, but it may also show praise and sheer joy. One of the most memorable stories in the Bible about lifting up hands is in Exodus 17:8–13:

> The Amalekites came and attacked the Israelites at Rephidim. Moses said to Joshua, "Choose some of our men and go out to fight the Amalekites. Tomorrow I will stand on top of the hill with the staff of God in my hands." So Joshua

fought the Amalekites as Moses had ordered, and Moses, Aaron and Hur went to the top of the hill. As long as Moses held up his hands, the Israelites were winning, but whenever he lowered his hands, the Amalekites were winning. When Moses' hands grew tired, they took a stone and put it under him and he sat on it. Aaron and Hur held his hands up—one on one side, one on the other—so that his hands remained steady till sunset. So Joshua overcame the Amalekite army with the sword.

Moses knew that the Israelites could not defeat the Amalekites without God, so he lifted up his hands in surrender to God's power, letting Him control the situation. When Moses dropped his hands, the Amalekites started winning, so Moses had Aaron and Hur hold up his hands, indicating that he knew that only God could defeat the enemy. Surrendering to God was what made the Israelites powerful.

When we lift our hands, we show God we are totally surrendered to Him. Perhaps too often, all of us face enemies, trials, and tribulations. And all too often, the world is a spiritual desert where our souls are starving and thirsty. However, when we make God our goal, not food and water, when we surrender to Him by lifting our hands, when we cling to Him as a child would, He takes our hands with the loving kindness that is His power and glory. He gives us the power to overcome when we admit that any victory is by Him alone.

We also praise the name of Jesus with lifted hands. He has taken our burdens, so we can lift our hands. Jesus gave us the free gift of salvation. Through Him we are adopted as children of God, complete with all the rights of the heirs of the King of Kings. We are baptized into His salvation and clothed in the righteousness of Christ, so God no longer sees us in our tattered garments.

We are no longer Jew or Gentile, slave or free, male or female, but true heirs that He takes and puts on his lap in loving-kindness.

So to become the King's children, we need to cling to Him, to surrender all, to lift up our hands. By clinging to Jesus, we are freed from the parched desert of life apart from Him in this fallen world. To put our hands in His, to be directed in His paths, makes us more than conquerors in Christ.

FILM TO FAITH

Watch this movie:

- *Rio Grande Ranger*

Ask:

- Why was it important in Hollywood Westerns, such as *Rio Grande Ranger*, for the people to surrender by lifting up their hands?
- Why did Moses lift up his hands to defeat the enemies of Israel?
- Why do many Christians lift up their hands in prayer, praise, and supplication?

Father, I often face serious difficulties and need your help. I surrender all to you and lift up my hands to reach out to you. Take my hands and empower me to be more than an overcomer in the name of Jesus Christ. Amen.

LOOKING AHEAD

What do you do when you are trapped and imprisoned by trials and tribulations, including the antipathy of a cliquish community? See the next devotion.

42

Let Us Sing Songs of Praise

MOVIES THAT INSPIRE

Paradise Road (mature audiences)

Joyeux Noël (Merry Christmas) (mature audiences)

What do you do when you are trapped and imprisoned by trials and tribulations, including the antipathy of a cliquish community?

Acts 16:25–34 gives us an example of this:

> About midnight Paul and Silas were praying and singing hymns to God, and the other prisoners were listening to them. Suddenly there was such a violent earthquake that the foundations of the prison were shaken. At once all the prison doors flew open, and everyone's chains came loose. The jailer woke up, and when he saw the prison doors open, he drew his sword and was about to kill himself because he thought the prisoners had escaped. But Paul shouted, "Don't harm yourself! We are all here!" The jailer called for lights, rushed in and fell trembling before Paul and Silas. He then brought them out and asked, "Sirs, what must I do to be saved?" They replied, "Believe in the Lord Jesus, and you will be saved—you and your household." Then they spoke the word of the Lord to him and to all the others in his house. At that hour of the night the jailer took them and washed their wounds; then immediately he and all his

household were baptized. The jailer brought them into his house and set a meal before them; he was filled with joy because he had come to believe in God—he and his whole household.

This is a radical suggestion. How could Paul and Silas sing hymns while they were in one of those horrific prisons? If you've toured the Middle East or read history books, you realize how dark, dingy, diseased, and rat-infested the prisons were; yet Paul and Silas were singing. As a result of their prayers and praise, the prison doors flew open, and the jailer and his family came to Christ.

It's interesting that the movie *Paradise Road* (1997), based on a true World War II story, is similar to the biblical story of Paul and Silas. Women and children are trying to escape the Japanese advance on Singapore. Their ship is bombed, and three major women characters are captured by the Japanese and put in a prison camp with a diverse variety of international women, from nurses to missionaries to high-society ladies.

It's hard to tell what was more miserable—this camp or the prison where Paul and Silas were. Two of the women decide to start a vocal orchestra. The Japanese had warned them against singing, and some of the women were beaten and tortured. They are prepared to beat the women again, but the women start their concert using their voices as instruments to produce beautiful music. The Japanese decide not to persecute them, and the women gain their freedom in a unique way by surviving the war. One of the women later came to the Annual Movieguide® Faith & Values Awards Gala.

So singing songs of praise in the midst of extreme adversity opens our life to God moving in a unique and powerful way.

Another great movie is the international production *Joyeux Noël* (*Merry Christmas*) about a famous incident in World War I during Christmas in 1914. The English, the French, and the Scots are facing the Germans across the trenches. The trench warfare consists of constant killing. On Christmas Eve, one famous German opera singer starts to sing "Silent Night" for the German troops, and a Scottish bagpiper joins him from the Allied trenches. Soon, nearly everyone is singing Christmas songs and praises to Jesus. The enemy soldiers come out of the trenches praying for each other, sharing pictures, playing games, and celebrating the birth of Christ. Of course, the next day the war starts again.

We live in a sinful and broken world, so we will always face trials and tribulations, but the Bible tells us many times to sing songs of praise, such as in Psalm 95:1–2: "Oh come, let us sing to the LORD; let us make a joyful noise to the rock of our salvation! Let us come into his presence with thanksgiving; let us make a joyful noise to him with songs of praise!" (ESV).

If we do, God will deliver us spiritually and often physically. Perhaps we are not in an ancient jail or in a war, but even if we are just trapped by trials, tribulations, and ill will, God will be there with us in our songs or praise.

FILM TO FAITH

Watch one or both of these movies:

- *Paradise Road* (1997) (mature audiences)
- *Joyeux Noël* (*Merry Christmas*) (mature audiences)

Ask:

- Why did the women in *Paradise Road* decide to create a vocal orchestra?

- How did the Japanese react?
- How did God deliver the women in *Paradise Road*?
- Why did the soldiers in *Joyeux Noël* join in the singing of "Silent Night"?
- How did God deliver the soldiers in *Joyeux Noël*?
- What happened the last time you sang songs of praise? Did it inspire you or encourage you to do something special to honor God or help other people?

Father, sometimes I feel imprisoned by trials, tribulations, and criticism, and sometimes I'm imprisoned in other various ways. Please fill my heart with joy and my mouth with songs of praise, so you show up and show me the way of deliverance. In Jesus' name, amen.

LOOKING AHEAD

What makes a family great? What makes a family movie great? See the next devotion.

43

God's Design for Family

MOVIES THAT INSPIRE
Swiss Family Robinson
The Incredibles

What makes a family great? What makes a family movie great?

Disney's 1960 classic *Swiss Family Robinson* is about a family who learns to pull together when shipwrecked on an island. It is a rare and fine example of a family functioning as a team to do things they couldn't do as individuals.

Considering the importance of family in society and the world, it's surprising how few movies feature an intact family working together to face the challenges in life. In *Swiss Family Robinson*, it's quite enjoyable to see how creative the family is in building a large home in a huge tree.

Psalm 127:3–5 tells us that children are a blessing of the Lord that makes us stronger: "Children are a heritage from the LORD, offspring a reward from him. Like arrows in the hands of a warrior are children born in one's youth. Blessed is the man whose quiver is full of them."

One of the best modern movies that exemplifies this truth is Pixar's popular animated movie *The Incredibles*. A family of superheroes learns that only together can they defeat the movie's great villain. Each family member has unique abilities that are needed in the course of the adventure.

Sadly, the mass media of entertainment in general has been hard on the family. That's why Pat Boone and I wrote *The Culture-Wise Family*. Families are being torn apart by worldviews that leave

God and His design for the family out of their stories. When people conclude that children don't need a father at home or that one's occupation comes above one's role in the family, society begins to crumble. Prisons are filled largely with young men from broken family situations where the father was absent. A healthy family passes on healthy values, as Proverbs 22:6 infers: "Train up a child in the way he should go, even when he is old he will not depart from it" (NASB).

Training is not the responsibility of the school or the church. They can and do assist, but the responsibility rests with parents (see Deuteronomy 6:4–9)—and it is more and more challenging in this mass-media age.

In the past, the primary influences on children were family, school, church, and friends. Today, children are inundated with media, most of which do not acknowledge God's love and wisdom. Without knowledge of God's plan for our life, it's easy to stray into very destructive behavior.

To train up a child in the way he should go is to train him or her in how to walk with God, how to sense His love and grace, and how to find His wonderful will for his or her life. We are each created unique, but God designed us to need each other and to work together. Like in *Swiss Family Robinson* and *The Incredibles*, our families face trials and tremendous stresses, but it's when we come together, combine our strengths, and trust in God that we're strongest.

The Bible is not a book of sweet family stories. It's full of stories of broken families that result in mayhem. We can learn from these stories just as we can learn from sad stories in our own lives. What we need to learn is to put God first and keep Him there.

Putting God first makes for the healthiest and strongest family, and it is very important in the choice of media, but this doesn't mean we watch nothing but sweet stories. It means that we discern and discuss. When we read the Bible story of David and

Bathsheba, we're not supposed to condone adultery and treachery. We learn of the horrible consequences of these things. We don't revel in David's wrongdoing; we learn from it.

Of course, this doesn't mean you should rush out to see disgusting movies so you can analyze them. It does mean that you should seek God's will regarding what you see, and be prepared to discuss as a family what can be learned from the movie or program.

FILM TO FAITH

Watch one or both of these movies:

- *Swiss Family Robinson*
- *The Incredibles*

Ask:

- What strengths did each family member have in *Swiss Family Robinson*?
- How important was unity in each movie?
- What was the greatest mistake made by Mr. Incredible?
- How important was Mr. Incredible's family to him? Why?
- What strengths do the members of your family have?
- How important is your family to you? Why?

Father, I thank you for how you designed the family. Help me to play the role in my family that you wish me to play. Give me wisdom and discernment on my choices of media. You know what's best for my family and me. Lord, may there be more and more movies and entertainment made that strengthen families, communities, and society by glorifying you and showing your love and grace.

LOOKING AHEAD

Have you ever made a prediction? See the next devotion.

44

His Script, His Drama, Your Story

MOVIES THAT INSPIRE

The Bible, TV miniseries (2013)

Dudley Do-Right (1999)

Have you ever made a prediction? Perhaps you found out that you have no ability to look into the future. Sometimes, based on best estimates and analysis, we can ascertain where things are going, but detailed revelations of the future are a gift from God.

This is one reason why Easter week is so incredible. The resurrection is not only the greatest story ever told about Jesus. As the TV special miniseries *The Bible* shows in visualizing the story of God's Word, Easter week is also a script that God wrote hundreds and even a thousand years before Jesus Christ, describing in detail this great drama that has two points—that we are forgiven indeed, and that Jesus is our Savior.

In every drama, there is conflict—or as the Greeks called it, *agon*, from which we get the words *protagonist*, *antagonist*, and *agony*. The conflict comes from the fact that the hero or protagonist will do anything to win the prize, and the villain or antagonist will do anything to stop him or her.

In early stage melodramas and Hollywood movies, the villain would tie the girl to the railroad tracks rather than see the hero win her hand in marriage. The 1999 movie *Dudley Do-Right* expands on this basic plot conflict. Jeopardy is something at stake, such as Nell (Sarah Jessica Parker) in *Dudley Do-Right*.

In the passion story of Jesus Christ, *you* are at stake. You are priceless, but you are fatally flawed. You've inherited a genetic disease. So the hero, Jesus, comes to provide the cure. In Genesis 22:8, it says God will provide the cure, the sacrificial Lamb. He replaces our broken spirit with His Spirit to redeem us and give us eternal life.

Psalm 22 is a clear script of what goes on at the crucifixion. It was written one thousand years before Jesus was born, and at least six hundred years before crucifixion was invented. Crucifixion is a labor-intensive, slow form of murder. It takes a carpenter to prepare the wood, someone to prepare the nails, and then a couple of people to nail the victim and raise him up on the cross.

Hundreds of years before this painful method of death was invented, God described it in detail. He says that Jesus' life would be poured out like water, just as happened when the centurion stuck the spear in Jesus' side and water poured out (John 19:34). Why water? Because it meant that Jesus was already dead; otherwise it would have been blood.

Psalm 22 also says that His hands and feet were pierced. Why?

Because when you commit a crime you have to pay the price, and when you break one of God's Ten Commandments, you have to pay the price. Since we have broken at least one of these commandments, we need to pay the price, but the good news is that Jesus paid the price for us.

In Isaiah 52 and 53, which are called the suffering servant passages, the prophet says that Jesus was pierced for our transgressions, but he also predicts that He was resurrected so that we can be saved.

On the road to Emmaus in Luke 24, two of Jesus' disciples were discouraged after the crucifixion. Jesus appeared to them and told them that if they had read God's script about the drama that was being played out, they would have known exactly what was happening and what was necessary for their salvation.

As Peter explained in Acts 10, God anointed Jesus with power to do good and to heal. After He was crucified, God raised Him up. He appeared many times to many people. He ate and drank with them. And everyone who believes in Him receives forgiveness.

So God's script was fulfilled: 1) when the crowd cheered on Palm Sunday because they wanted a king and prayed for prosperity, but Jesus offered them a suffering servant who would give them salvation; 2) when Judas was filled with greed and sold Jesus for thirty pieces of silver; 3) when Jesus was abandoned by his best friends, including Peter; 4) when He was wrongly convicted; 5) when He was beaten and cursed; 6) when Jesus took all our judgments on Himself on the Cross; and 7) when Jesus was resurrected as the sign and the seal of our salvation.

All of this was foretold, foreordained for you. The evidence demands a verdict. The drama was written for you to confess that "He is risen, indeed; He is risen for me."

FILM TO FAITH

Watch one or both of these movies:

- *The Bible*, TV miniseries (2013)
- *Dudley Do-Right* (1999)

Ask:

- How does the TV miniseries *The Bible* show that God foretold the Easter week drama of Jesus Christ hundreds and even a thousand years before the events of the passion?

- How does *Dudley Do-Right* show the basic elements of dramatic conflict?
- What do the Easter week events mean for us?
- Why is the story of Jesus Christ called the greatest story ever told?

Father, I pray that you would move me with the drama of the passion of Jesus Christ and transform my life eternally, in Jesus' name. Amen.

LOOKING AHEAD

How should we deal with the political culture? See the next devotion.

45

A Holy Calling

By Rob McCoy[15]

MOVIE THAT INSPIRES

Amazing Grace

How should we deal with the political culture?

The movie *Amazing Grace* reawakens our mind to the idea that we can and should make a difference in a suffering world of sin. Amid today's desire for superheroes and fantasy, it is refreshing to witness a visual retelling of the real-life heroic story of William Wilberforce and his monumental achievement of stopping the legal slave trade in the British Empire.

The movie challenged my apathy and pietism and made me realize I must not think that a holy calling can only be a pulpit ministry. As a result of this movie, I realized that a holy calling can be found in the halls of government.

There is a profound scene in *Amazing Grace* where the Reverend John Newton (a former slave ship captain played by Albert Finney) encourages William Wilberforce (Ioan Gruffudd) to engage the enemy of human souls in the halls of government to "blow their [the slave traders'] filthy ships out of the water." I was so moved by this scene that it inspired me, as a pastor, to run for public office.

---

15 Editor's note: Rob McCoy has been senior pastor at GodSpeak Calvary Chapel in Thousand Oaks, California, for over sixteen years. Elected in 2015, he currently serves as a Thousand Oaks City Councilman. Pastor Rob is married to Michelle, "my greatest blessing," and has five children. They live in Newbury Park, California.

Pursuing this endeavor resulted in pushback from those I thought would be my greatest supporters—other pastors. Instead, they believed that engagement in politics was a dirty business at best. My reply to pastors was, and continues to be, that church work is dirty business. They would respond by saying they were tired of always having to vote for the lesser of two evils, to which my response is, "Unless Jesus is running for office, we will always be voting for the lesser of two evils."

Amazing Grace allowed me to see that God's work can and must be done in all of culture, especially in the halls of government. In a day and age where we, as a culture, no longer understand the biblical ideas of how freedom and liberty apply to government, this movie inspired me to gain a whole new perspective.

In the movie, Newton warned Wilberforce of how intense and difficult this calling would be, and he could not have been more accurate. I have ministered behind the pulpit for over twenty years, during which I never faced the kind of trials and persecution I have faced while running for public office.

Good government happens with good people, and we as Christians must engage this culture with the love and wisdom of Christ. First Timothy 2 admonishes us to pray for kings and those in authority that we might live quiet and peaceful lives in all godliness and reverence.

This admonition has caused me, on numerous occasions, to ask a room full of pastors to list by name the local officials (city council and school board) whom they have been called to pray for, and the main issues these officials are contending with. My question is always met with profound silence, as few, if any, pastors know the names of their local officials. Apathy will enslave people, and though engagement in politics requires effort and education, we owe it to humanity to engage.

Amazing Grace will inspire and empower you toward action. Beware, persecution will follow, regardless, so may the love of Christ empower you to this holy calling.

FILM TO FAITH

Watch this movie:

- *Amazing Grace*

Ask:

- How did John Newton convince William Wilberforce to stay in Parliament?
- What difference did it make for William Wilberforce to stay in Parliament?
- What is a holy calling?
- What has God called you to do?

Father, the world seems to be spiraling out of control. Give me a holy calling to redeem an area of life for the benefit of your kingdom, to the honor and glory of your name, Jesus Christ. Amen.

Reel to Real
Movie Index

* Mature audiences only
For reviews of these movies, please go to movieguide.org.

Bibliography

Baehr, Ted. *How to Succeed in Hollywood (Without Losing Your Soul)*. WND Books, 2011.

Baehr, Ted, and James Baehr. *Narnia Beckons*. Nashville: Broadman & Holman Publishers, 2005.

Baehr, Ted, and Pat Boone. *The Culture-Wise Family*. Ventura, CA: Regal Books, 2007.

Baehr, Ted, and Tom Snyder. *Frodo & Harry: Understanding Visual Media and Its Impact on Our Lives*. Camarillo, CA: Media-Wise Publishing, 2008.

Acknowledgments

For their fine work, I acknowledge the efforts of Serena Miller, David Sluka, and Tom Snyder, and contributors Mary Driscoll, Pastor Jaime Loya, Pastor Rob McCoy, David Outten, and Pastor Bruce Zachary. I also would like to acknowledge the Movieguide® Board of Directors, Board of Reference, supporters, and fans, as well as the Hollywood entertainment-industry filmmakers, leaders, and talents who have produced movies and television shows with faith and values that encourage and uplift biblical principles.

Prayer for Discernment and Wisdom

Father, you created us in your image to create and to communicate. You told us that we are to be in the world but not of the world. So we pray for you to give us discernment and wisdom so we seek the good, the true, and the beautiful in art and entertainment, and avoid the bad. We also pray that we will see your truth in the movies and entertainment that proclaim your biblical principles, and that we will avoid movies and entertainment that reject these principles. Have your way with us, Lord Jesus Christ. Come, Holy Spirit. Amen.